Praise for Hinges

"The church in America has spent years trying to get the community to come through our doors. Now, a book about how to swing the door the other way—out! In this practical volume, the authors have given practical insights and approaches that will help leaders and congregations who are willing know what they must do to become externally focused and internally strong!"

> —Reggie McNeal, speaker and best-selling author, *Missional Renaissance* and *Kingdom Come*

"*Hinges* is a key resource for leaders who are serious about helping their congregation ... reach out to the community. Drawing on years of both research and experience with their Transforming Churches Network, the authors help inwardly-focused congregations shift to the adventure of mission just outside their front doors."

> —Greg Finke, Executive Director, Dwelling 1:14; author of *Joining Jesus on His Mission: How to be an Everyday Missionary*

"God the Father sent His son. Jesus sent his disciples. The New Testament teaches us that in our 'going' we are to make disciples. Yet many churches in our nation are waiting for people to come to them, rather than going to those who need Jesus. *Hinges* teaches pastors and congregations how to be 'going' churches not 'waiting' churches. This book will help your congregation to effectively obey God's command to 'go.'"

> —Dr. Paul D. Borden, author, *Make or Break Your Church in 365 Days*

"I'm tired of hearing how the church is dying. I'm ready to do something about it. This book puts God back at the helm of our churches where he should have been all along. Thank you for writing a book that gives practical and relevant ways to be a missional church."

> —Melanie Smollen, President, Faith Perceptions

"*Hinges* is a practical guide into exhilarating participation in the Gospel reaching more people. I hope we church leaders will use *Hinges* as one benchmark in our ongoing efforts to reach more people for Jesus."

> —Dr. Dale A. Meyer, President, Concordia Seminary

Hinges

Opening Your Church's Doors
to the Community

Terry Tieman
David Born
Dwight Marable

TCN
TRANSFORMING
CHURCHES NETWORK

©2015 by Transforming Churches Network

Published by
Transforming Churches Network
1160 Vickery Ln. Ste #1, Cordova, TN 38016
901-757-9700
www.tcnprocess.com

All rights reserved. No part of this publication may be reproduced, stored in a re-
trieval system, or transmitted in any form or by any means—for example, electronic,
photocopy, recording—without the prior written permission of the publisher. The
only exception is brief quotations in printed reviews.

Unless otherwise indicated, Scripture quotations are from the Holy Bible, New International Version ®. NIV®. Copyright © 1973, 1978, 1984, 2011 by Biblica, Inc. ™
Used by permission of Zondervan. All rights reserved worldwide. www.zondervan.
com.

For more information, please contact:
terry@transformingchurchesnetwork.org

Dedication

David J. Born,

our partner in ministry and brother in Christ, who opened doors for the Gospel everywhere he went.

A true "Renaissance Man," David was extraordinarily capable yet amazingly humble. His friendship, wisdom and gifted service will be sorely missed.

David's legacy of equipping God's people to reach those who need to know Jesus will live on through this book and those who read it.

Table of Contents

Introduction

During the final stages of completing this book, David Born had an accident while repairing his home and passed on to be with the Lord. We miss our friend and colleague deeply. His family will feel the loss even more as they will be without a husband, father and grandfather. Our TCN partners who received the benefits of his wisdom, felt his passion for reaching the unreached and enjoyed his practical instruction will also have an empty place in their hearts.

David was a carpenter as well as a pastor, missionary and theologian. He knew how to build a home, restoring and renewing properties as well as congregations. David was a master at patiently teaching leaders and churches how to apply the Hinge principles we learned in our research. He was effective at helping pastors grow as leaders, which invariably meant integrating into their calling the critical role of equipping God's people as missionaries in a post-church culture. The pastors who sat with David in Learning Communities will never view the church as an institution to be maintained, but rather as the hands, feet and voice of the Gospel whose purpose and calling is to serve, love and witness to those who need to know Christ.

I (Dwight) began working with David to train congregations in small-group evangelism right after the turn of the millennium. About that time, our church body adopted some very bold goals, including sharing the Gospel of Jesus Christ with 100 million people around the world by the five hundredth anniversary of the Lutheran Reformation in 2017. In addition to church planting, a major strategy for accomplishing these goals was revitalizing 2,000 churches in North America. For a denomination that peaked in membership in the mid-1970's and in which the vast majority of its congregations (85% by some estimates) are plateaued or declining in annual worship attendance, turning around one-third of its 6,000 churches is more than a challenge.

The denomination asked me (Dwight) to help them develop a strategy for reaching this enormous goal. I conducted an extensive research project that was translated into our Hinge Factors, becoming the foundation of our work. At the same time, Terry was working on revitalizing congregations in his district. Based on his successes in his district, Terry was invited to become the first Director of Revitalization for The Lutheran Church—Missouri Synod. During this time, David was also asked to become a Regional Director for the national church body, focusing on helping congregations reach their communities with the Gospel.

The three of us combined our efforts and worked with congregations across the country to pilot the Hinge Factors. Worship attendance in the 90 churches in this national pilot grew by an average of 12%. As a result, the denomination suggested that we form a non-profit organization to focus on helping churches. With their support, we formed Transforming Churches Network (TCN). Being a small organization enables us to be free from national bureaucracies while allowing us to stay nimble and responsive to congregations, pastors and judicatory leaders. The purpose of TCN was, and is, to help any interested congregation to transition from being an inward-focused church to one that is having an impact on their community for the Gospel.

Opening Doors for the Gospel

The beauty of developing the TCN network was that it became a national learning community. TCN developed training tools and processes based on quantitative and qualitative research. As we have implemented these processes over the past seven years, we continually learned from feedback from the grassroots level, modified our tools and improved. Some 1000 congregations later, we now can provide practical resources based on extensive research and proven results with real people and real situations.

This is not a one-size-fits-all model. We are not asking you to come to our mega church, or for that matter to come to any congregation of any size, and learn how to imitate us. Rather, TCN offers a principle-centered approach that focuses on proven best practices. These practices must be contextualized in your unique congregation and community. Your leaders will need to experiment and learn together how the Lord will use you in your environment. The principles and practices will work, regardless of location, ethnicity or congregational age and stage.

This book is intended to be a primer for pastors and church leaders to gain some new insights and learn practices that can enable them to open doors to their community with the Gospel of Jesus Christ. We know that Jesus is the only Way into the church, but there are many church doors that lead back out to the community where lost people can still be found. He said, "I tell you, open your eyes and look at the fields! They are ripe for harvest" (John 4:35). As we obey, he will help us find that ripe harvest in our community and fulfill His purposes for our congregations.

1

Opening
New Doors

In the opening scene of the movie *Get Smart*, Maxwell Smart, played by Steve Carrell, walks through a series of mechanical doors to accomplish his mission. As soon as he passes through a door, it slams shut behind him, cutting off the path. As we look at the church landscape in America, we can see a tragically similar situation. Where once the people walked through wide-open doors to hear the Gospel of Christ, now that same church finds those doors shutting. In many cases, these doors are shutting in a literal way as churches close at an alarming rate. But in even more situations, the doors are closing in a figurative way. Even though God's people have tried very hard to keep the church open to the community, fewer and fewer people from outside seem to be coming in.

Stories abound about how churches are experiencing this door-closing phenomenon. These stories go deeper than statistics or abstract descriptions about the church in America. These are personal stories about love for God and love for God's church. Over the last decade, we have been working with these churches, helping them take steps to a new future. The following three stories illustrate some of the more common experiences we have encountered about how people experience doors closing.

Story #1: Pastor Matt.

After another three-hour meeting, he was losing hope. In the first half of his ministry, he preached the Gospel on Sundays, took care of the sick and shut-ins, taught confirmation to the children and tried not to do anything stupid. He had been a competent, if not charismatic, minister as all of the parishes in which he served had grown. People only left the church when they died or moved.

Now things were different. People, especially the younger families with children, were leaving to attend the new non-denominational church across town. While he publicly referred to it as "Gospel Lite," he secretly wished he could replicate some of their programs.

After attending a church revitalization seminar, he had a new plan that promised that the best days were yet to come. However, the initial euphoria had worn off after three months, especially when several established leaders declared that the newly formed Board of Directors was simply a group of the pastor's cronies. Then they started boycotting worship and stopped giving their offerings. That's why Pastor Matt had been attending so many long meetings.

What is Pastor Matt to do?

Story #2: First Church.

Located in a small, Midwestern town, the people of First Church were celebrating its centennial, but with mixed feelings. People were making statements like, "We're happy to celebrate 100 years of God's grace, but I wonder if anyone will still be here to celebrate 125."

They had a good picture of reality. The town was in decline, and as a result so was the church. No new houses had been built in the last ten years, and businesses had closed, turning a bustling downtown into a ghost town.

First Church had just hired a recent seminary graduate named Pastor Green. The problem is that he wanted to change everything. Since Pastor Green had grown up in a large church in the suburbs, he didn't

know much about rural culture. Like most seminary graduates, he had
received excellent training in theology and pastoral care, but he was
given little to nothing of practical value in the areas of leadership and
outreach or the nuts and bolts of how to turn around a dying church.

What is First Church to do?

Story #3: Grandma Martha.

As this faithful matriarch worshiped, she thought, "Things could
not have been going better." They had just remodeled the sanctuary
and expanded the school and offices through a multi-million dollar
capital campaign; attendance and giving were
up by over a third in the past five years; a young,
dynamic youth pastor had joined the staff; and
there was even talk of expanding to a second
campus. Grace was a thriving, mid-sized, suburban congregation, reaching the upwardly-mobile
families that were moving into the middle-class
subdivisions springing up all around it. Everyone
was happy, happy, happy! The year was 1985.

**The neighbor-
hood around
the church
had changed
significantly
in three
decades.**

Martha is a grandmother now, and her grandchildren were not
attending church with her. They were on the soccer field. The truth
is that Martha's own children had stopped going to church with her
just after confirmation, and they had graduated from college doubting
the existence of God. So when it came to a choice between attending
church and soccer practice, there wasn't much of a contest. The neighborhood around the church had changed significantly in three decades;
the new neighbors were not the kind of people that had attended Grace
Church in the past. But it was more than that; society had changed.
Grace, like every church in North America found itself as a lone voice
in a secular culture which in its sophistication and self-importance had
left the church behind.

Grandma Martha and her beloved church were nothing more than
a vestige of a bygone culture. She fretted about what had become of
her family and worried about the future of the church. Most of all, she
was conflicted over a Jesus who is for everyone in every generation, but

who was shut out of the lives of so many people, including the ones she loved the most.

What is Grandma Martha to do?

Much has been written about the decline or even what some call the death of the church in America. The statistical reports on these matters are overwhelming. More than 80% of all the churches in North America are plateaued or declining in worship attendance. Billions of dollars are spent annually on theological education, seminary training, seminars, books and workshops and yet there are still 300,000 churches that are struggling to impact their communities in a meaningful way. The Southern Baptist Convention projects that it will lose 15,000 churches by 2025; the Roman Catholic Church, in recent years, experienced a decline in membership for the first time in its history. Lyle Schaller has observed that no mainline denomination has ever seen a significant turnaround once it has started to decline. Only one county in the U.S. has a higher percentage of Christians today than a decade ago. Only about 15% of all Americans can be found in a house of worship on a Sunday morning. The negative stats roll over us like a tidal wave. Even worse, all of these statistics represent real people who will spend eternity apart from the love and care of Jesus Christ unless something changes dramatically.

The doors to the church are not open to the community like they once were. The challenges we face hit us hard. We love God and we love God's bride. We love how God has used the church to change our lives, how it has provided belonging, transformation and even hope. But church doors are closing.

What are we to do?

Hope for the Church

Most churches across America can share similar stories about closing doors. Must we idly stand by and watch it happen? We can feel so powerless. The potential reality of seeing our beloved churches close can fill us with anger, frustration and sadness. Even worse, growing numbers of people in our very neighborhoods are clueless about the eternal love and saving grace of our Lord Jesus Christ and would be lost forever without coming to terms with the consequences of their sin apart from Jesus' saving love. But, it doesn't have to be that way!

Trinity opened its doors in a storefront in 1941, and they had no trouble keeping the doors open. Ten years later, they built a 250-seat sanctuary, and by 1961 they were filling it three times every Sunday. After 40 years of open doors to the community, a trend was becoming obvious. The pattern was not dramatic, but when this church called us a few years ago, church attendance was down to 25. No one could point to any one thing that had shifted or to any major issue that had caused the exodus. It was just looking for hope when no one was coming through their doors any more.

After 35 years of slow decline, Trinity finally embarked upon a new journey when they engaged us to help them take some new steps on their journey. Abandoning its expectation that they could still attract people in their community with their worship opportunities and programs, and armed with a new vision to build new relationships in their community by meeting some of their real needs, the people of Trinity traded in their victim mentality for an attitude of godly hope.

The Lord sent them a new pastor who enthusiastically shared their new missional vision. Under his leadership they were able to focus on a number of new initiatives designed to serve their community. Moreover, this new pastor was able to model outreach behaviors which empowered the members to gain confidence and competence in touching the lives of their neighbors. They stopped worrying about their declining church attendance and concentrated on building God's Kingdom by sharing the love of Jesus with new people. As they did this, the numbers started turning around all by themselves.

When we seek to build the Kingdom first, all of the organizational decline that consumes us starts to turn around.

After about three years, new hope came through newly opened doors. With the support and guidance of Transforming Churches Network (TCN), sixty people had been added to the life of Trinity. Those 25 people who had contacted us learned anew that Jesus is true to his promise that if we seek the Kingdom of God and his righteousness, all the other things we desire will be added as well (Matthew 6:33). This is true for the church as an organization as well as it is true for God's people as individuals. When we seek to build the Kingdom first, all of the organizational decline that consumes us starts to turn around. This is a fundamental philosophy of ministry of TCN.

One pastor confessed that when his church gave up trying to survive as an organization and began sharing the Gospel with their neighbors, a whole new life came forth like spring flowers after a long and dismal winter. As Jesus taught, "Whoever finds their life will lose it, and whoever loses their life for my sake will find it" (Matthew 10:39). This is how hope is found. This is how the doors of the church are opened.

Hope in God

Over the past decade, we at TCN have worked with over a thousand churches across North America, and the vast majority has experienced revitalization. Our goal is not to provide empty promises and dreams of hope, but to actually offer a practical path that puts you on a journey of opening doors. This is God's path of hope for your church, not that of any man.

God's mission is to seek and save lost people (Luke 19:10) through His Son Jesus.

God's people are captured anew by the heart of God. Our Heavenly Father's passion is that "all people be saved and come to a knowledge of the truth" (1 Timothy 2:4). That is why he sent His Son Jesus to be our Savior, living a perfect life in our place and dying on the cross to pay the price for our sin. And that is why he established the Church and promised that it would be "so expansive … that not even the gates of hell will be able to keep it out" (Matthew 16:18 MSG). God's mission is to seek and save lost people (Luke 19:10) through His Son Jesus. He has called His body the church, those of us who are his followers, to go into all the world and carry out this holy mission of making disciples (Matthew 28:18-20).

Even though, somewhere along the way, many of us got so involved in the institution of the church that seeking the lost was moved to a back burner, this can change. When we seek God's Spirit so that our hearts begin to resemble the loving and compassionate heart of God in Christ Jesus, we truly get our priorities straight concerning our care about lost people and reaching them with the Gospel. When we are compelled by Christ's love (2 Corinthians 5:14-15) for us, we can find a new path to live out that love through our church and in our community.

When people are motivated by Jesus' love and empowered by the Holy Spirit in our churches, there is absolutely nothing that God cannot accomplish through His Church, including lost people pouring in the Church's doors as a result of God's people pouring out through those doors into the community.

How that happens is explained very simply in John's Gospel, where Jesus says: "I am the door; if anyone enters through Me, he will be saved, and will go in and out and find pasture" (John 10:9 NASB). The only way to salvation and thus, entrance into the Invisible Church, is through him. He is the only Door into the Church. Evangelical churches have always taught salvation by grace alone through faith in Christ.

What is often misunderstood, however, is what we are supposed to do after we become Christians and how we are to live out our faith. Our natural inclination is to stay inside the church where it is safe and warm and comfortable. But that is not the illustration that the Good Shepherd paints for us. Jesus says that two things happen to His sheep when they enter through him. First, they will be saved, and second, they will go in and out and find pasture. They don't stay inside the sheep pen. Rather, they continue to follow the Good Shepherd wherever he goes, including back out into the pasture. What that means for us as Jesus' disciples is that once we start following the Good Shepherd, we will continue to follow him wherever he leads us, including back out into the world.

Doors are opened when God's people, who have been brought inside the Church through the power of the Holy Spirit working through the Word, go outside to show and to tell others about the Good Shepherd. It happens when congregations get out of their buildings and out into their communities. It happens when the sheep understand that while there is only one Way into the Church, there are many doors that lead back out to where huge flocks of lost sheep can still be found!

It can happen and will happen for you and your congregation if you take the step of faith into the future, reach out to your community and let the light of Christ shine through you and your people. This passion drives what we do in our services to local congregations. The following chapters will give you proven principles and best practices, illuminating the path ahead for bringing the light of Jesus into hopeless and struggling lives.

Discussion Questions

1. To which of the three stories in the opening section can you best relate? Why? Does it seem to you that the doors of your church are closing? Why or why not?

2. What has your church done in recent months or years to try to stem the tide of decline? What has worked? What hasn't?

3. Urgency and hope go together like a hand in a glove. Without urgency, a complacent church will not wake up and make necessary changes. Without hope, the tendency is to simply give up and die. On a scale of 1 to 10 (with 1 being "everyone has already given up and is simply waiting for the official closure of the church" and 10 being "we are so hopeful that God will direct a major turn around in the next few months that we are already planning a celebration"), where would you rate your church right now? Why?

4. Look up the following Bible passages and share the hope they give you for the future, both for you personally and for your church: 1 Timothy 2:4; Matthew 16:18; Luke 19:10; Matthew 28:18-20; 2 Corinthians 5:14-15

5. According to John 10:9, what are we supposed to do after we become Christians and how we are to live out our faith? What specific thing(s) can you do this week to help another "sheep" go out and "find pasture"?

Activity: Consider doing this prayer activity as you work through this book, either during your group time or by yourself at home, or both.

   1. Share about a few lost people you know in your web of relationships. List them in the space on the next page:

2. Think of relatives first, then friends, neighbors, work associates and acquaintances.

3. Pray for the people you have identified by name.

4. Pray that God would open their hearts for you to share the Gospel with them.

5. Ask for opportunities to befriend these people and share the Good News of Jesus with them this next week.

2

Hinges that Open Doors to the Community

Pastor Matt, First Church and Grandma Martha are all worried that the doors of their churches would soon be closing. How do they go from concern to action? How does the mission of God get carried out? How can congregations emerge from their buildings, programs and institutions and effectively engage their communities with the power of the Gospel?

Pastor Bob found a way to address his concerns about these issues. In a mid-sized town in Arkansas, he saw a struggling church shift to one that opens its doors. Annual adult confirmations increased from one to 32, baptisms from six to 25. He saw this occur as the church walked through a process of developing a unified vision that focused the church on Christ's Great Commission to reach those outside the church.

After Pastor Bob contacted TCN, we began with an evaluation of the church, which resulted in some practical prescriptions to help the church become more focused on outreach. One prescription was that the congregation plan and implement six outreach events in a year to demonstrate their seriousness about reaching out to those who may not know Christ. As a result they developed several successful activities to get members out into the community. Prayer walking was an initiative where church members went to residential areas and apartment communities and, while walking through the community, prayed for the residents inside each home. When they were finished praying, the church member left a door hanger that read: "A member of Hope Church came by and prayed for you today. If you have any additional prayer needs, please let us know."

They also invited the entire community to attend their "Party in the Park" event, which was a fun and free day of activities that included band performances, children's games and fun treats. For Halloween, the church invited community members to their Trunk or Treat event in the church parking lot. Church members decorated their vehicles and served candy and treats out of their vehicles' trunks. This was great fun and a safe way for children in the community to celebrate Halloween.

In addition to increasing the church's community presence, these events helped bring in 57 new members to the congregation in their first year of revitalization. The process created an atmosphere of cooperation and unity that Pastor Bob had never experienced before. The congregation, staff and pastor all working together to become a mission-focused church has had a tremendous impact on everything they do. Even the church's Monday morning staff meetings have become a time of celebration as they focus on the amazing work that God is doing among them.

Such stories can be repeated in churches across America. Historically, however, the church has demonstrated an unwillingness and inability to change, even incrementally. While it can be debated why this is so, experts agree that there are two powerful forces for inducing meaningful change. Either the current situation becomes so unbearable, or there is a new option that is so compelling and positive that it cannot be resisted. While it would not be difficult to build a case for the former (see the preceding chapter), we believe that when churches see a compelling option for the future that they will embrace a new way forward. This is the premise of the work we do with churches, which is based on what we call the 8 Hinges that Open Doors to the Community. These Hinges offer the hope for the needed change based on the promise of producing real help and hope for American pastors and churches. This life-changing hope is born from demonstrable results through a process that has already proven its effectiveness in many churches across America.

It is our premise that every church has the potential to open their doors to the community. Tools and processes are needed that fit the gifts and culture of the local church. Those tools and processes are at the heart of what we do, and we believe they can be used by any pastor and church. Hope can spring in the hearts of every struggling church in America by discovering and implementing these door-opening devices. It is our desire to help transform churches all across North America by showing them how to open doors into their community with the Good News of Jesus.

Finding the Right Hinges

Through the years, there has been a myriad of lists of characteristics offered to church leaders telling them what it takes to be a healthy church. Interviews have been performed. Endless surveys have been completed and tabulated. Complex statistical analyses have been run. And from this, church doctors have told us what it means for a church to be healthy.

While our questions are related to church health, they are also quite distinctive. More than just identifying the characteristics of churches that are healthy, we have sought to know the key characteristics of churches that effectively empower church members to engage their communities with the Gospel. In other words, our research has focused on identifying the key factors, what we call Hinges, that shifted inwardly-focused congregations into churches that opened their doors to the community.

To find these Hinges, we surveyed over

We have sought to know the key characteristics of churches that effectively empower church members to engage their communities with the Gospel.

1,000 people in small to medium-sized churches in America. We processed this information through extensive statistical analysis, and we were able to determine the factors that lead to turning a church from an inward focus to an outward one. More specifically, we sought to understand the actions that lead to growing attendance, to new baptisms and to more new attenders from the community. The sophisticated processes that we have used have been guided by experts in this kind of statistical analysis.[1]

The results of the research conclusively indicate that there are eight behavioral drivers that will transform a plateaued or dying inwardly-focused church. The research demonstrates which factors, or "Hinges," lead to things like new Christians getting baptized, new people participating in weekly worship and overall growth in the congregation. Activating these Hinges results in meaningful community impact with opportunities for demonstrating and sharing the love of Jesus Christ with those who need to hear and experience the message of the Gospel.

Overview of the 8 Hinges

The eight Hinges fall into two different groups of four. The first group applies to leadership, especially to the characteristics and actions of the senior pastor of the local congregation. The second four refer to the characteristics of the congregation as a whole. The first four Hinges open the pastoral leadership door, while the second group opens the congregational door.

The two sets of Hinges work in tandem. For example, one congregation discovered that their weakest Hinges were Bridge-Building Leadership (Pastor Factor) and Community Outreach (Church Factor), while their strongest Hinges were Visionary Leadership (Pastor) and Inspiring Worship (Church). This discovery led to the pastor and congregation leveraging their strengths to improve their weaknesses.

Specifically, the pastor, who is a gifted visionary and strong leader, began preaching on the necessity of engaging the community with the Gospel. At the same time, he modeled what it would look like by block-

PASTOR FACTORS

CONGREGATION FACTORS

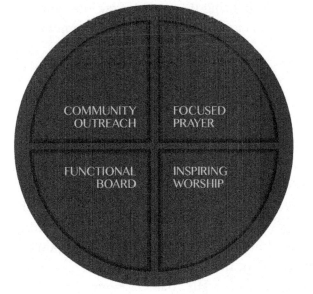

ing time on his calendar to get to know his neighbors by inviting them to coffee, a meal, a ballgame or just hanging out with them in the yard. He helped organize a neighborhood block party. By using his strength (Visionary Leadership) to address the congregation's weakness (Community Outreach) and by also demonstrating his willingness to grow, the pastor quickly made a huge impact on the entire congregation.

One example has been the implementation of regular Service Project Sundays. On these Sundays, after a brief worship service, the entire congregation goes out into the community and demonstrates the love of Jesus by engaging in a number of servant activities. Those activities include things like cleaning up vacant lots, handing out bottles of water to thirsty people and cleaning restrooms at area gas stations.

During this last activity, the congregation discovered that there is a growing homeless population in the area near the church. This discovery led to the congregation establishing a flourishing homeless ministry, with some of these men and families coming to Christ and being baptized. Best of all, the congregation is seeing more people from the community coming to worship, being baptized and instructed in the faith, and then going back out into the community and sharing the love of Jesus with their friends and neighbors. By understanding their own Hinge Factors and utilizing them effectively, this church has made a huge missional impact on their surrounding community. Here are the eight Hinges:

Hinge #1: Empowering God's People for Works of Service

Empowering people is the primary Hinge that opens the door for maximum missional impact in the community. Without this Hinge in place, the leaders of the congregation will be weak or ineffective. All of the other Hinges are directly linked to this pivotal factor, because the equipping and releasing of others for ministry is required for the effective implementation of the other seven factors. This is especially true in regard to the senior pastor. His ability to equip and empower others to engage in mission and ministry will often determine a church's ability to experience meaningful transformation.

The three key skills of empowerment are 1. encouragement, 2. delegation and 3. equipping. Through the tools and processes we have developed, we invest a great deal of energy in senior pastors so that they can develop the skills to get this Hinge in excellent working order.

All of the other Hinges are directly linked to this pivotal factor.

Hinge #2: Personal Leadership

How can a leader empower and guide the people of a congregation if he isn't able to demonstrate sound leadership in his own life? Of course, the answer is that he can't, at least not very effectively. A leader must be able to manage his own life well if he is going to lead others. He must embrace habits and disciplines that will help him live in a healthy and God-pleasing way, particularly in the areas of physical, mental, spiritual and relational development. Our work with leaders focuses on helping them in the development of time management skills, spiritual disciplines and relational health.

Hinge #3: Visionary Leadership

Vision must be in the driver's seat as the church ventures out into the community. Vision—"a clear picture of a preferred future"—isn't discovered on a mountaintop or handed to leaders engraved on tablets of stone. Rather, it comes by seeking the heart of God and seeing where he is already working in the community (John 5:16-20). However, discerning God's vision isn't even the hardest part; communicating that vision is! This development of this Hinge helps pastors use multiple communication systems to cast an outwardly-focused vision and create urgency within the hearts and minds of their people.

There are four components in the life cycle of a church. They are vision, relationships, ministries and structure. Of these, vision takes pride of place, because it determines how the other three play out. Vision reveals who we are and where we are going. Vision impacts the values, the character and activities of a congregation. Amongst the complexity of a church organization composed of many different people doing all kinds of different things, vision is the one overarching direction upon which everyone agrees. Vision is what we see the congregation looking like in a future preferred by all, and all participants in the vision can see themselves in an exciting, or at least satisfying, place in that future.

Hinge #4: Bridge-Building Leadership

In order to open doors to the community, it is crucial for the church's key leaders to get out of the office and engage the community. For many church professionals and volunteer leaders who are accustomed to leading from the office or the boardroom, this can be scary and intimidating. Yet, there is no better way to learn about the needs, the culture and the people in a local community than by actually meeting with them and talking to them. This Hinge is all about the pastor and other key leaders modeling for the congregation how to connect the church to the community by assessing needs, building bridges, meeting people and forming connections. Through this modeling process, leaders gain credibility as they invite the congregation to go along with them in building relationships with and serving the needs of the lost and unreached people in their own neighborhoods.

Hinge #5: Community Outreach

This powerful Hinge swings the church's doors open for God's people to become incarnational disciple makers. Jesus said to His first disciples, "I will make you fishers of men" (Mark 1:17). Today, he might say to us, "You have to go fishing to catch a fish!" Serving people opens their hearts to new relationships and the Word of Christ. The church is not limited to a piece of property and a building. The scattered church lives, works and plays in a specific place. Whether it is the inner city or exurbia or some place in between, there we are. The places where we find ourselves set the context in which we can demonstrate the love of Christ, build relationships that open hearts to the Word of Christ, sow the seeds of the Gospel and reap an eternal harvest. This is community outreach and has been since the days that Christ walked the streets of Jerusalem. This Hinge is about how to do this in a way that empowers and encourages God's people.

Hinge #6: Functional Board

Our research revealed that church boards are vital to the transformational process. This can be done in a variety of models as there are a number of governance structures and approaches that have proven to work well. While not subscribing to any one model of governance, a healthy and robust board is immensely valuable for a pastor and a congregation. For a board to consistently function well, it must balance two dynamic components: 1. Attend to the spiritual needs of a congregation (matters of "being"), and 2. Review and bring meaningful accountability to the management of the ministry (matters related to "doing"). Functional Boards must support the pastor's leadership role while providing protection for the congregation through boundary principles. The board makes sure that the pastor has all the resources and support that is needed in order to accomplish the mission and ministry of the church. In turn, the pastor is held accountable for the vision of the church. The application of these broad principles is congregationally specific and must be contextualized by the stakeholders of the church for transformation to occur.

> **The board makes sure that the pastor has all the resources and support that is needed in order to accomplish the mission and ministry of the church.**

Hinge #7: Focused Prayer

Focused prayer is an emphasis on prayer that incorporates intercession for those who need to know Christ. There are a number of dimensions related to this goal, and it cannot be accomplished by the pastor or leaders alone. St. Augustine once said, "Pray as though everything depended on God. Work as though everything depended on you." Prayer for the lost and unchurched by name and prayer for the church's vision to become reality cannot be overlooked. Prayer during the times of worship, in prayer groups, during board and staff meetings and in private devotions will have impact. As St. Paul says, "Pray continually" (1 Thessalonians 5:17).

Hinge #8: Inspiring Worship

Seekers attend church hoping to make friends and connect with God in a way that is meaningful to them. Mature believers are often looking to go "deeper" in their knowledge and experience of a personal, yet sovereign, Lord and Savior. There is no "one size fits all" worship experience. Both formal and informal worship may provide a way for a wide variety of people to sense the presence of God. Passionate and professional, enthusiastic and contemplative, historical and contextual, or challenging and comforting are all poles on a wide spectrum of approaches that may facilitate individuals in experiencing God's presence in a time of worship.

Inspiring Worship services need to be experiences where the preaching, music and atmosphere appeal to a growing number of people from the community. There are a number of dimensions related to this goal, and they cannot be accomplished by the pastor or worship leader alone. With this in mind, TCN strongly encourages that this Hinge be developed through a team-building experience with those who could become a worship team or a worship planning team.

Conclusion

All of these Hinges work together to move people out into the community and transform the life of the church. When the pastor and other leaders are Empowering God's People, it impacts the Focused Prayer life of the congregation, which means the church will be more effective in praying for the lost and the unreached. The church will have more Inspiring Worship as people are engaged in ministry and works of service and building relationships with new people.

As people are praying for the lost, people will be more inclined to actually go out and spend time with them.

When you impact prayer and worship, Community Outreach will be stimulated. As people are praying for the lost, people will be more inclined to actually go out and spend time with them. And if people are worshiping in such a way that God is really impacting their lives, they will be more inclined to be more involved in Community Outreach. And on it goes!

All eight Hinges are connected to one another, as the illustration below shows. This diagram will be used at the beginning of each chapter that addresses one the eight Hinges to keep the inter-connected nature of these factors before you.

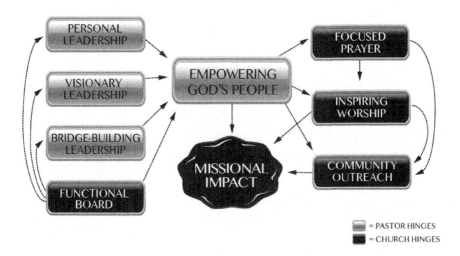

= PASTOR HINGES
= CHURCH HINGES

Installing these Hinges to open doors depends upon the development of new skills. Much like shooting a left-handed lay-up, installing a sink or tweeting, these are skills that almost anyone can develop. While no matter how many hours you spend in the gym shooting lay-ups, you will likely never become the next Michael Jordan; and no matter how many bathroom floors you flood, you will never be mistaken for Bob Vila. Even so, practice will improve your abilities.

The same is true for developing your personal and congregational leadership and outreach skills. You may never be recognized on the street as a mega-church pastor or make the Top Ten List of Fastest Growing Churches. However, you can make a greater missional impact on your community and improve your effectiveness in sharing the love of Jesus Christ with more people who need to hear and experience the life-changing message of the Gospel.

While there are tons of important skills that are needed in the church today, these eight focus on the areas that actually open doors and turn churches around. In addition, these are eight skills that can be applied in any kind and size of a church. Let's explore how you can put these Hinges into motion, starting with the center of the diagram above, Empowering God's People.

Discussion Questions

1. Do you agree with experts who say that there are two powerful forces for inducing meaningful change: "either the current situation becomes so unbearable or there is a new option that is so compelling and positive that it cannot be resisted"? Which of the two is more likely to occur in your church? Why?

2. How open do you think your congregation is to understanding its Hinge Factors and utilizing them effectively? How open do you think your pastor is?

3. Define each of the 8 Hinge Factors in your own words.

4. Of the 4 Pastor Factors, which would you consider to be the strongest in your ministry? Which ones need to be improved?

5. Of the 4 Church Factors, which would you consider to be the strongest in your ministry? Which need to be improved?

3

Empowering
God's People
Part 1

"It's unsinkable," they said. In 1912, the greatest ship ever constructed was launched with the assumption that nothing could touch it. However, on its inaugural voyage, that which the engineers said was impossible happened. The unsinkable ship sank. It sank not because of what was visible, but because it struck what could not be seen. Since only ten percent of an iceberg, the proverbial "tip of the iceberg" sits above the water line, the mighty Titanic was destroyed by colliding with what could not be seen: the 90 percent of the iceberg that lies hidden beneath the surface.

As churches seek to launch out and open doors to the community, the issues that most often get in the way lie beneath the surface. Our churches are surrounded by icebergs, which all include important issues we don't confront regularly. It's not so much about adopting the right strategy or program for opening doors. That's the stuff we can see. It's about the hidden issues that undermine new ventures in mission when they are left unaddressed.

Iceberg issues are the things that keep a church from being what God intends his people to be. They prevent the church from getting involved in ministry as they lock pastors in patterns that hinder them from leading the people of the church into true transformation. These iceberg issues freeze the Hinges that open the doors to the community and keep the church from making a greater impact.

The most significant and dangerous icebergs are related to the role of the pastor in leading the church.
Over the last several years, we have discovered that the most significant and dangerous icebergs are related to the role of the pastor in leading the church. For the most part, people want their pastor to lead their churches into new life that they might better influence their world for Christ. However, they also want the pastor to continue fulfilling all the traditional expectations of pastors from prior generations: expectations that he run the church organization, keeping peace among the members, that he be the theologian who prepares excellent sermons, that he is the primary caregiver for all the members and that he is the effective teacher of young and old alike. The problem is that this traditional role of the pastor, which is more like the role of a chaplain for the members, and the role of the pastor as missional leader are almost mutually exclusive.

In contrast, we know from our research that the key to opening the doors of the church to the community is located in the ability and the

freedom of the pastor to empower God's people for works of service. In fact this Hinge is central to opening up the other seven, as is illustrated by the diagram on the previous page.

What does Empowering God's People mean? Why is it so important to the life of the church? And what stands in the way of this Hinge? These are core questions that this chapter will address. While most people in our churches would say that they want to see this kind of empowering happen, the hidden issues remain at the deeper levels of priorities and values, threatening to undermine our efforts to fulfill our calling from God and purpose as church. In this chapter, we will define the Hinge of Empowerment. In the next chapter, we will provide some practical steps for putting it into practice.

Why Empowerment Is So Crucial?

Our first-hand experience and our statistical research have demonstrated conclusively that this Hinge makes or breaks a church's ability to open doors to the community. When the pastor empowers people for ministry, the Hinges of the church creak open because all of the other Hinges are directly connected back to this one. Without this Hinge in working order, the other seven Hinges will freeze up.

Let's break down the specific ways that Empowerment changes things. First, this pivotal Hinge has a direct effect on the missional impact of a local congregation. When God's people are empowered to do works of service doors are opened to the community. People are equipped as individuals to get outside the church and intentionally meet and form relationships with people who need to hear the Gospel. This is about shifting from the pastor doing all of the work of the ministry to sharing that work with others.

As illustrated on the next page, Community Outreach is the second Hinge that has a direct impact upon opening doors to the church, but the ability of a church to implement this factor flows out of the Hinge of Empowerment. Outreach has the greatest impact in the short run. In fact, we have found that congregations that do four to six commu-

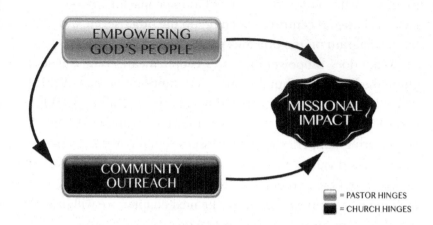

nity outreach activities per year will almost always have a significant missional impact on their community, including experiencing growth and conversions (More on this in chapter 8). So the question is, how do we get the people of our congregation excited enough to go and do six community outreach events every year? The answer is found in the Empowerment Hinge, as it mobilizes people to actually get out and do the Hinge of Community Outreach. This requires us to think about how we might create a culture of empowerment.

Empowerment in the New Testament

The Apostle Paul established the biblical foundation for Empowering God's People:

So Christ himself gave the apostles, the prophets, the evangelists, the pastors and teachers, to equip his people for works of service, so that the body of Christ may be built up until we all reach unity in the faith and in the knowledge of the Son of God and become mature, attaining to the whole measure of the fullness of Christ (Ephesians 4:11-13).

The Incarnation of Jesus culminated in the Resurrection after which he empowered his followers to form the church. After his ascension, Christ gave gifts to that church through the promised Holy Spirit, empowering his people to continue on. According to the text above, Jesus gave apostles, prophets, evangelists, pastors and teachers to do the work of equipping the church.

God gave leaders to the church. The way that the church carries out the calling is through the leadership. It's not by the leadership doing the ministry. Verse 12 makes it clear that the leaders are "to equip his people for works of service." The calling is for the entire church, not just the clergy. The role of leadership is to equip, "so that the body of Christ may be built up." Equipping is about putting the right tools in the right people's hands and teaching them how to use them. This is about "building up" or "encouraging," which is the translation of the Greek word *oikodomeo*. The root of this word is *oikos*, which we translate as home, house or family. The job of leadership is to build up the people of God as God's household or family.

When we say "empower God's people" we are referring to the equipping of people for works of service. Whom do we serve? We serve all, those within the church and those in the community. It's about showing the love of Jesus to other people. It's the Great Commandment, and the Great Commission. Loving the Lord our God with all our heart, soul, strength, and mind and our neighbor as ourselves. And then also going and making disciples.

When we say "empower God's people" we are referring to the equipping of people for works of service.

One way to illustrate how the Hinge of Empowering God's People works is to think in terms of a coach who is also a player. Baseball coaches don't get out on the field and play the game. They rally the troops. They help the players be the very best players they can be. Some of them are generalist coaches who oversee everything. Then there are specialists, a hitting coach, a fielding coach and position coaches. The job of the coach is to help others fulfill their calling. The difference with our calling as pastors is that we also get to have fun and participate in the ministry alongside those we are coaching.

Creating a Culture of Empowerment

It's easy to talk about the role of equipping from a biblical perspective, but actually doing this in the midst of the realities that we face as pastors in our churches is another thing. This is where the icebergs sneak up on us. Comedian Garrison Keillor once described the state of a typical Lutheran church in Minnesota by using the Latin motto *summus quod summus*, which means "we are what we are." The motto is a product of a culture which accepts present limitations because all the baggage is just too overwhelming to change.

Culture shapes what goes on beneath the surface of the iceberg, affecting everything the people of the church do. Every church has a culture which has formed over the years by the people's values, attitudes and practices. Every pastor and congregation must wrestle with the aspects of its culture that will support the opening of doors into the community, along with those aspects that are apt to resist it.

As I (Terry) was coaching a pastor of a church just outside of Kansas City, it became apparent that the expectations of his congregation were well beyond what any human being could sustain. I asked him for a copy of his job description, and he produced a seven-page document. Besides "ensuring the Word of God is preached and that the sacraments are administered according to Christ's command," it also stated, "the senior pastor is the primary leader in the areas of worship, administration, pastoral care, stewardship, outreach and education." Under the pastoral care section, it even went so far as to stipulate that he administer the birthday-care program.

This describes the iceberg that undermines the crucial Hinge of Empowerment, and it's pervasive. When we ask people at seminars to list the real expectations of the pastor, participants usually state:

- preaching
- visiting the sick
- nurturing the saints
- leading Bible studies
- counseling the hurting

- leading the organization
- administering the details of church life
- weddings
- funerals
- baptismal ceremonies
- leading worship
- working with the board

Sometimes people add things like cutting the lawn, repairing the plumbing and cleaning bathrooms. We can certainly recall doing a lot of these types of things in our early years in the ministry! Even though all of this may take 60 to 80 hours a week, the pastor also must make sure that his children and his wife are modeling what it means to be a Christian family.

The job of the pastor, in the eyes of the average parishioner, is to do the work of ministry, all of the work of ministry. It's the job of the pastor to do the outreach, the inreach, the proclamation and the shepherding of the flock. This is the iceberg. We have built this expectation.

So if it's the pastor's job to do ministry, then what's the role of the members of the congregation? We say that we want people to offer their time, talents and treasures, but how does it really work? If we were to be honest with ourselves, the way we do church is set up so that people are expected to attend, to pray, to put money in the plate and to refrain from complaining too much about the job the pastor is doing.

> **The job of the pastor, in the eyes of the average parishioner, is to do the work of ministry, all of the work of ministry.**

We have developed a way of doing church, a hidden culture, which puts all of the pressure on the senior pastor. Over the last decade, we have facilitated what we call Learning Communities (see chapter 12 for more on these experiences) where pastors gather in a small group for the sake of mutual support, learning and discussion about how to lead a church into transformation. The biggest problem is that some pastors don't show up for the meetings, even though they tell us how beneficial they are. When we ask them why they miss, they tell us that they are too busy and usually it's an emergency. We are amazed at how many emergencies crop up, some of which sound ridiculous when you think about it. One pastor shared, "I had to drive a hundred miles today to go visit somebody in the hospital. And there was nobody else that could go visit this person because they needed me." Really? Nobody else could have done this?

When we look further at these expectations, we can see just how big the hidden part of the iceberg is. What lies beneath the actions of driving 100 miles to visit someone in the hospital? What motivates pastors to put in 80 hours a week? What drives them to do all the ministry while everyone else sits and watches? The answers to these questions lie at the heart of why equipping and empowering God's people for works of service does not get done.

From our experience and from hundreds of conversations with pastors, we've discovered a disturbing reality. Many pastors get life from the silent implication of their parishioners: "This church could not function without you. If you ever left, pastor, we don't know what we'd do." Even though they've had 27 pastors, and they've always done just fine, congregations enable their pastors to over-function (and often get frustrated or even burn out), while the members sit idly by, wondering why their pastor looks so haggard. At the same time, pastors tend to have a secret desire to be needed.

Of course this is nothing new. Through the centuries the pastor or priest was one of the most, if not the most, revered and honored individuals in the parish. None had been educated like him. None had traveled as he had. None could speak as he could. And of course, none had direct access to God quite like he did. Today, many pastors continue to hold on to the iceberg because it gives a sense of fulfillment and importance. So the iceberg remains, ever growing and never revealed.

When we hold on to this iceberg, we will not see the fruit of Empowering God's People. The doors of the church will remain shut. And we can continue to expect the same results in our churches that we have experienced over the last twenty years. But when we begin to lead differently, we also see different results. We have seen this over and over in our work with churches.

We need not settle for Garrison Keillor's observation of the church that aims for being little more (or less) than it has been. The status quo of the culture of the past need not be the culture of the future. God empowers his people to do the works of love and service because they are inspired through the worship, inspired by the prayer, inspired by the study of God's Word and inspired by the hope of reaching people with the Gospel. Inspiration from the Holy Spirit of Jesus is contagious as it moves through pastors and leaders to the people. This creates a new kind of culture, one that recognizes that all power comes from the Holy Spirit who inspires new attitudes about service and discipleship within all of us, opening doors of God's church to the world.

> **The status quo of the culture of the past need not be the culture of the future.**

Empowering a New Future

Perhaps the best way to summarize the Hinge of Empowering God's People is with a story from early in TCN's work as an organization.

St. Mark's was a declining, aging urban church in the Mid-South. After undergoing a consultation, the leadership was advised to do a series of Community Outreach events as a way to build momentum toward becoming an outward-focused congregation. (We will talk more about this in chapter 8.)

The first step was to target a group of underserved people in their community. They chose to work with a local fire station where they already had some connections. This outreach fit in well with their stated vision of "giving the Bread of Life to our community and the world in Word and deed."

The first event was a Valentine's dinner for the firemen and EMTs from the station they had adopted. Twelve firemen attended the dinner and 33 air pumps were given out, with the extra pumps taken to the firehouse for the men on duty. The air pumps were bought from a supply company for just a few dollars apiece. Now, one of the fire fighters attends the church every Sunday. The exciting part is that he often arrives in a fire truck or EMT vehicle and almost always brings a trainee with him. Two of those trainees are now in an adult confirmation class. The first time he arrived in his fire truck, some of the members were afraid the church was on fire. Actually, something was starting to catch fire, as the enthusiasm of the people of St. Mark's grew with each successive event. The total cost of the first event was $100, a small investment with a great return.

The second event was a yard sale. 250 people attended the event and 50 prospect cards were filled out. The incentive to fill out the card was a prize drawing. Most of the participants were lower income people from the community who were hesitant to fill out the card until they were told that the drawing was free.

The yard sale was on a Saturday, and the prize drawing was held the next morning after the regular Sunday morning worship service. A woman and two of her children attended the service on Sunday and the drawing; her sister won a $50 gas card. Now the woman from that first Sunday, her three children, her sister (who won the gas card) and her mother all attend worship and are in the membership class. Total cost of the event was $185 for ten gift cards; again a modest cost to the church that produced wonderful results.

The third event was a diabetes workshop, sponsored by Methodist Hospital attended by 41 people from the community. The members were intentional about meeting these people and relating to them.

The fourth event was a Thanksgiving Basket distribution. Working with the Red Cross and the local fire station, church members got a list of names of fire victims from the previous year. Ten families were identified, and all were given a large basket of food that was taken to the families' homes the night before Thanksgiving. These families were touched by this act of kindness and began to think of the church as their spiritual home, even though they had never attended before.

The fifth event was called Operation Christmas Child. All of the fire victims' names and Christmas lists were gathered and put under a special Christmas tree decorated in the narthex at the church. Thirty-five presents were purchased and sitting under the tree on the Sunday before Christmas. The families were all invited to come to a special Christmas dinner, where they received their presents, and the children got to sit on Santa's knee and have their picture taken. Thirty-five people came to the dinner.

Of course, they were all invited to come back on Christmas Eve to worship the newborn Messiah. Twelve came back for that service. In fact, 50 of the 150 people in worship on Christmas Eve were first-time guests, including 16 children who were invited to play in the hand-bell choir. The director had invited them to come just a half hour before the start of the service for rehearsal. She knew that most of these children would not be able to come for regular practice, because they did not have anyone to bring them or they were simply not used to being asked to be reliable. According to all accounts, they played beautifully; in fact, many said it was the most meaningful Christmas worship service they had ever attended.

Less than a year after that first Valentine's Day dinner was served, the pastor's prospect list grew from five to 219, several people were baptized, new families were attending worship regularly and the optimism of the congregation had gone off the charts. What happened?

At first glance, it appears that the key was simply conducting a series of Community Outreach events and activities. But a closer inspection reveals that it was really all about the Empowerment of People to do ministry. During that year, the pastor of St. Mark's totally shifted the way that he did ministry. Instead of spending most of his time "doing" the ministry, as he had done for decades, he shifted his time and effort to "equipping" others to do ministry. After their new vision was established, he included it in his preaching, bulletins and newsletters. He talked about the vision at church meetings and with every individual member he met. In each of the outreach activities, he was the catalyst for recruiting, training and overseeing others who actually planned, conducted and led the events. He also modeled outreach behaviors at each event. He told the members that if there wasn't interaction between the members and people from the community at the outreach events and they didn't get any new names and contact information for the prospect list, the event would be a failure. Afterwards, he told the moving story of how long-time members with tears in their eyes had said the community outreach events had been the most meaningful things they had ever done at St. Mark's.

Isn't it amazing what God can do when his people are empowered to use their gifts and talents?

Isn't it amazing what God can do when his people are empowered to use their gifts and talents? The question we face as leaders is "What do pastors and leaders do differently in order to experience what they did at St. Mark's?" It goes far deeper than just implementing some outreach events. This is what we will discuss in the next chapter.

Discussion Questions

1. The mighty Titanic was destroyed by colliding with what could not be seen. In much the same way, hidden issues that float under the surface damage churches that want to reach out and open doors to the community. What are some of the "iceberg issues" that are keeping your church from being what God intends it to be?

2. Do you think that it is true that the most significant and dangerous icebergs are related to the role of the pastor in leading the church? Why or why not?

3. In your church, what is the role and expectations of the pastor? What is the role and expectations of a member? What is a disciple? How much are the specific roles and expectations we have for one another determined by culture and experience? By Scriptures? What is the connection between pastors, members and disciples? For a hint, turn to Matthew 28:18-20.

4. Based on Ephesians 4:11-12 and your discussion above, do you agree or disagree with this statement: "The primary emphasis of the pastor must be shifted from chaplain to missionary"? Why or why not?

5. Would you like to see the pastor and staff of your church spend more of their time developing God's people through coaching, equipping, mentoring and training? If that were to happen, what would be the implications for your church? For your community?

4

Empowering
God's People
Part 2

When pastors empower God's people, it leads directly to open doors. But there's more going on than the direct influence of the pastor. As illustrated by the story at the end of the previous chapter, empowerment of leaders has a direct impact upon the Hinge Factor of Community Outreach. The point is obvious: a church cannot do community outreach events without leaders.

In addition, Empowering impacts the prayer life of your congregation. The church will become more effective in praying for the lost and the unreached. The Worship Hinge also opens up as a direct result of Empowerment. Worship services will be more inspiring as leaders are equipped and as prayer increases.

Then all of this leads to missional impact, that is new conversions, baptisms and more attenders in church. The diagram on the next page shows how the Empowerment of God's People through encouragement to pray and inspiring worship has a direct correlation to the growth of the mission, as well as an impact upon Community Outreach which, in turn, grows the mission.

When the Hinge Factors of Focused Prayer and Inspiring Worship

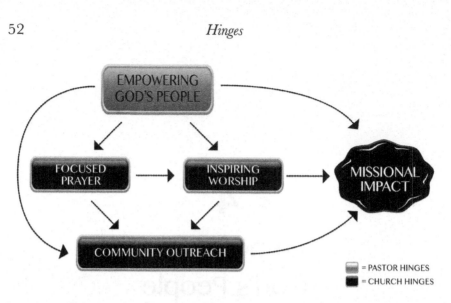

increase, Community Outreach increases. As people are praying for the lost they are more inclined to actually go out and spend time with them. And if you're worshiping in such a way that God is really impacting your life and the Spirit is really powerful in your heart, people are more willing to get involved in Community Outreach. If the Holy Spirit is the ultimate Empowerer, prayer focused on the mission will communicate to the Lord our desire to serve and our dependence upon his power to put it into practice. And it seems obvious that the inspiration and teaching we receive as we worship will generate power to serve.

Empowering God's People is about pastors learning a new way of leading by experimenting their way forward into a new reality. This releases pastors from having to do all the ministry while others watch and evaluate. This involves the development of empowering skills, specifically, encouragement, delegation and equipping.

Skill #1: Encouragement

The most outstanding ministries depend upon people working in their areas of passion and compassion. However, our thinking tends to begin with slots that need filling and then we go and find willing souls. "We need six Sunday School teachers, and we only have three who agreed to serve. Bob is loyal. Let's ask him." Bob thinks, "I'm not good with kids, but the church has a need. I'll do my best." Bob has passion for repairing cars and wonders if there are people in the community who cannot afford to pay for minor repairs or an oil change. He could get enthusiastic about that. Alas, that passion will have to stay on the shelf because Bob is putting so much energy into being a good soldier, doing what he does not enjoy.

Pete works for FedEx at the headquarters in Memphis, Tennessee. Five years ago, he traveled to Columbia, South America as a part of his work. While there, he toured an orphanage and fell in love with the kids. Now several times a year, he takes groups of people from his church and from all over the country to visit this orphanage and sponsor these kids.

Churches are full of people who are passionate about specific people and specific kinds of work. Often these people are directed to committee work and administrative details in the church organization. How much better would it be for the mission and for the people of passion if they were engaged in making a difference, perhaps an eternal difference, in the lives of people in their community? As we will testify in our chapter on Vision, many new people may come into the church because they are compelled by its vision of serving the community. These people are gifts whom God sends to a church to further its mission. Empowering leaders will help these people discover their passion and help them to fulfill roles that embrace it. If, on the other hand, we see them as helping us with our organizational needs and do not empower them to serve in the area of their passion, they will quickly move on to serve elsewhere.

Empowering leaders will help these people discover their passion and help them to fulfill roles that embrace it.

Working with people of passion, especially those who are new to the organization, will not always be easy. Their new ideas may not fit well with the status quo, and they will defend them passionately. It will be easy for the traditional leadership to get impatient with these people or dismiss them as counter-cultural. A principle we find ourselves repeating is "Protect gadflies and oddballs."[1] Every organization encounters people who are regarded as annoying, and some of them may be just that, but many may be passionate people, eager to push the church into its next level of mission.

Skill #2: Delegation

Delegation is not only a key to aligning people of passion with appropriate areas of service, but it is also an essential skill which will protect a pastor's well-being and help him exercise his priorities as a visionary and pastoral leader.

For pastors who are learning to delegate, we have some specific counsel. First we encourage him to keep a log of everything he does every hour for a week, and with a coach to evaluate each item, mak-

No pastor can add this to everything else he is doing.

ing distinctions between things that empower from things that maintain the institution. Then, with vision in hand, the pastor and the coach set priorities and eliminate things that do not further the vision. Finally a delegation strategy for addressing priorities should be developed.

When we first talk about Empowering God's People with pastors, they often look at us with a burdened face, as if the job of the pastor is not big enough already. They assume that all of this is now added on top of the list of responsibilities outlined in the previous chapter. However no pastor can add this to everything else he is doing.

When I (Terry) was a pastor in Fort Smith, Arkansas, I found that I could no longer make all the hospital visits and lead the church well. I, along with the elder board, created four hospital visitation teams, each comprised of four people that we trained to make hospital visits. They would alternate one week on, one week off, between the two hospitals.

Over a period of years, I instructed all the new members that they should not expect me to visit them in the hospital. We would tell them that they would be cared for, but that care would come from a small group or an elder. Then I'd tell them that they would get better care than from a pastor, and they did. Of course, I learned that it was easier to visit some of the long-time members because they would stir up more problems than it was worth if I did not, but those people were few in number.

Skill #3: Equipping

The passage from Ephesians 4 says that leaders were given to the church by Jesus "to equip his people for works of service, so that the body of Christ may be built up until we all reach unity in the faith and in the knowledge of the Son of God and become mature, attaining to the whole measure of the fullness of Christ." God's people need to be encouraged, and at the same time they need real skills and resources supporting them if they are to be effective in the church's mission of making disciples. Some of these have to do with "people skills" and skills that will help people in the community with specific needs. More basic equipping depends upon knowing and believing the message we hope to share, as well as our overall spiritual viability.

Biblical Teaching
People have to be in the Word in order to be empowered. This is a basic principle of the Christian faith. For the most part, in the churches we have worked with over the years, we have found that they do a good job of teaching the Bible. People are in the Word and have a relatively good knowledge of the Scriptures. Knowledge is not the problem. However, working out the implications of the Word for the here and now is a different matter.

Biblical teaching goes beyond simply expounding on the meaning of particular passages. It helps people discover what the ideas being taught mean for life today. For instance, it's one thing to teach on Ephesians 4 and the role of leaders in the church of the first century, but what does it say to us, not only in our

The Word of God is the means he chose to instruct, encourage and equip us as His ambassadors in the world.

current age, but in our specific setting as a congregation as well? How do I understand myself and my role as a leader in my church? The Word of God is the means he chose to instruct, encourage and equip us as His ambassadors in the world. We have to know it, and we have to know how to apply it. And because it is a living Word, its implications for our ministry are constantly growing as we grow in our faithfulness and service. More than knowing the content of Scripture, its application to our lives is a lifetime endeavor.

Knowing the content of the Gospel is also a piece of the equipping process. When we form relationships with people outside the church, we trust that sooner or later the stage will be set for us to share our faith in Jesus with them. How to say this, what all the relevant words should be, how to field potential questions—these are all-important things in which we receive competence as we are taught sound biblical information.

Bridge-Building

We have said that coaches do not play on the field, and that pastors are like coaches. We have also said that a pastor delegates so that he is not overburdened by doing all the work himself. A pastor who is an effective evangelist may be able to grow the numbers in his congregation by five percent per year all by himself, but to significantly grow the Kingdom of God and the church as well, to make a significant dent in the numbers of people who are being lost, we will need every member of the church participating on the field with a passion. Here is where pastors need to play on the field as well, as the most effective way to equip people for the mission is by modeling. Pastors build relationships with unchurched people so they can show their members that it can be done and how it can be done. Ultimately, pastors tell their people that they are out on the mission field not because it is a part of their pastoral duties but because they are also members of the Body of Christ.

Pastors build relationships with unchurched people so they can show their members that it can be done and how it can be done.

Training

The most obvious way to equip people is training, which need not be lengthy or overly detailed—people get the picture fairly quickly. Certainly, there are programs that can be used to train people in various ministries, especially in more specialized areas like stewardship, pastoral care, Christian education and so forth. Perhaps the best and simplest way to do this, however, is through immediate mentoring. The key here is that whenever you are engaged in any kind of ministry, always make sure that you are doing it with a partner. Never do anything alone! And instruct your mentee to be looking for someone that they can train and mentor as well. Pretty soon you will have a whole chain of people involved, all in various stages of growth and with varying degrees of skill. A simple formula for doing this is:

1) I ask you to join me in a ministry task;
2) I do the ministry and you watch;
3) We do it together;
4) You do it and I watch;
5) You do it with a new person that you have recruited;
6) I go on to another ministry task, while checking on you from time to time.

Using this simple formula, ministry can continue to multiply exponentially. Give them some training and then release them to do their ministry. They don't need to be micro-managed. Draw clear boundaries and tell them, "as long as you stay inside these boundaries, go do your ministry. Then tell us what you're doing so we can celebrate with you."

Real-Life Experiences

In the book *Same Kind of Different as Me*, a conversation between the authors, Ron, a wealthy art dealer, and Denver, a homeless man who has lived in poverty most of his life, reveals the need to move beyond just knowing the Bible and into the next step of real-life experiences. Denver asked Ron, "Do all you Christians go to church? Do all you

Christians go to Bible study?" Ron responded, "Well, not everybody. A lot of people do." Denver responded, "Well, when you start a *Bible doing group* you let me know and I'll come."[2] (emphasis added.)

This is exactly what Jesus did with his disciples. Very early in his ministry, he pushed them far beyond any talk about theory and theology and into the realm of experience.

> After this the Lord appointed 72 others and sent them on ahead of him, two by two, into every town and place where he himself was about to go. And he said to them, "The harvest is plentiful but the laborers are few. Therefore pray earnestly to the Lord of the harvest to send out laborers into his harvest. Go on your way. Behold, I am sending you out as lambs in the midst of wolves. Carry no moneybag, no knapsack, no sandals, and greet no one on the road. Whatever house you enter, first say 'Peace be to this house'. And if a son of peace is there your peace will rest upon him but if not it will return to you. Remain in the same house, eating and drinking what they provide, for the laborer deserves his wages. Do not go from house to house. Whenever you enter a town and they receive you eat what is set before you. Heal the sick and say to them, 'The kingdom of God has come near to you.' But whenever you enter a town and they do not receive you go into its streets and say 'Even the dust of your town that clings to our feet we wipe off against you.' Nevertheless, know this: that the kingdom of God has come near. I tell you, it will be more bearable on that day for Sodom than for that town" (Luke 10:1-12).

Jesus' disciples had very little experience in healing the sick, casting out demons and proclaiming the good news of the Kingdom. Sure, they had been with Jesus for a while and watched him do these things, but as far as any formal training or actually doing these things themselves, they were novices at best. What was Jesus' solution? Give them some real-life experience, sending them "out as lambs in the midst of wolves." Perhaps we should consider more discipleship training like that today.

A pastor in Oregon preached on the need to engage their community with the gospel, but he went beyond preaching. Most people hear a sermon on the Great Commission and get excited about it in the moment, but as soon as they get out the door of the church and go to lunch with church friends, they've forgotten what the sermon was about. Whatever excitement and motivation they had is gone because they did not have an immediate opportunity to put it into practice.

What was Jesus' solution? Give them real-life experience, sending them "out as lambs in the midst of wolves."

In his sermon he talked about how the disciples were bringing the little children to Jesus. "Unless you become like one of these little ones, you cannot enter into the kingdom of heaven." At the end of the sermon, he said, "I want all of you to imagine that you have this little child in your arms. Think about who that little child might be. I want you to put a face on that little child. And I want it to be the face of the people in your community or in your own personal life who do not know Jesus as their Savior. Write their names on your bulletin now. Pray for those people this week, and when God gives you the opportunity, show the love of Jesus to that individual. When we return next Sunday, I will ask you to write down your experience so that we can share them with the rest of the church."

In another church, they started something called "Service Project Sunday," which they do twice a year. On one such Sunday, they had a 30-minute service after which they released everyone to go out and serve in one of seven projects that have been planned in advance.

One group decided to clean toilets for area gas stations. They instructed 20 people who were divided into five groups of four: "You've got one hour. Clean as many bathrooms as you can in one hour." Then they all came back and shared what happened.

On one occasion, a group went to a small gas station less than a mile from the church building. The manager asked why they would want to clean his nasty bathroom. They said, "It is very simple. We want to show the love of Jesus to the neighbors in our community. We're just a mile up the road. We want to show that we care about our community by doing this." And finally he said, "Okay, that would be great, go do it." They asked, "Can we have the key?" He laughed and said, "There's no key to the restroom. We don't lock the doors, because the homeless people would tear the doors off the hinges."

The people from the church were shocked. They were unaware that there was a homeless population in that area of town. After they cleaned that one bathroom for an hour, Jeff—this man is six feet six inches tall, a tough fireman—was in tears. He said, "This is wrong. There are homeless people living within a mile of our church, and we didn't know about it."

Over the next week, they discussed the situation and prayed about how they should respond. One person said, "The only way that we can figure out how to minister to the homeless is to get to know them."

They returned to the gas station a couple weeks later with toothpaste, toothbrushes and shampoo. When they arrived, there was a crowd of homeless people, including Shorty and Bill, a man with one arm. The next Sunday, Shorty started coming to their church and has been coming ever since. He has been confirmed and is a faithful member. Bill has also gotten involved with the church.

This all started because Jeff had a real-life experience that changed his heart. Because his heart was changed, he was ready to do something about it. That's where the pastor and other leaders were so important, because they helped equip and train him and others. Until people have these kinds of experiences they're not going to have that change of heart and get engaged in doing something that's really going to make a difference in the community.

Discussion Questions

1. How does Empowering God's People impact the prayer life of a congregation? The worship life? How do these three Hinges (Empowerment, Focused Prayer and Inspiring Worship) affect Community
Outreach? How do they all interact together to impact the mission
of the church?

2. Does your church have "people of passion"? Can you name some of
them right now? How might these passionate people be encouraged
to be mobilized for service?

3. Read Matthew 16:24-25; Luke 11:1-2; Matthew 11:28-30; Mark
1:35-38; and Nehemiah 1:1-4. What do these Bible passages have to
say about how Jesus went about the task of making disciples? What
do they say about the role of the pastor and empowering God's people for ministry?

4. Brainstorm some ways that your church could provide some real life
experiences to give people an opportunity to discover where they
could begin serving.

5. Personal Reflection Questions:
    • What are some ways that I could be more intentional about
    releasing others to try something new?
    • Who needs my permission to take a risk?
    • What existing meetings, groups, or ministries, which I am cur-
    rently doing myself, could I delegate to someone else, in whole
    or in part?
    • What new ministry would I like to be empowered to do?
    • Write out the names of five or six potential servants below:

Interlude
Empowering
Empowerment

In case you missed the point, let us repeat it here again: Empowering God's People is crucial to the future of your church. The pastor cannot do it alone. However, neither can the pastor simply pull himself up by his bootstraps and just start doing the Hinge of Empowering. Of course effort and making choices are part of the journey, but our research has demonstrated that there are specific Hinges that shape a pastors ability to empower others. The diagram on the next page illustrates this point.

Leadership begins with self, the Hinge of Personal Leadership (discussed in chapter 5). This includes things like growing in your own faith, staying in the Word, praying regularly, taking care of yourself emotionally, physically and mentally, managing your time well, etc. If you don't do those things well, then it's going to be pretty tough to be able to lead a congregation or to impact the lives of other people.

Visionary Leadership (see chapter 6) is the second thing that helps clear the path for Empowerment. Vision is simply being able to articulate a clear and preferred future. Where are we headed? Where is God leading us? What would God have us to do in the next three to five

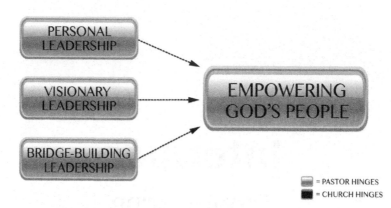

years? When you know where God wants you to go as a congregation, it is easier to get other people excited about the same vision. When a congregation shares such a vision, they will be greatly encouraged each time the leadership points them to it with clarity and shows how that vision is being accomplished. In this regard, it is essential that some more straightforward vision goals be completed as soon as possible as "early wins," by providing concrete evidence that will encourage the members.

It's next to impossible to get others to do something the pastor is not willing to do himself. Actions speak louder than words.

Thirdly, when a pastor is out in the community, building relationships with ordinary people and participating in mission, he can talk about the vision from his own experience (more on Bridge-Building Leadership in chapter 7). If the pastor is building relationships with lost and unreached people, he can talk about that on a personal basis from the pulpit, in Bible study, in conversation and in meetings. It becomes a whole lot easier to get people excited about what is being modeled. It's next to impossible to get others to do something the pastor is not willing to do himself. Actions speak louder than words.

The Role of the Board

Empowering God's People is connected to one more thing, the church board (chapter 9). How the leadership board operates directly influences the pastor's ability to empower the congregation.

When a church has a well functioning board, one that serves within an effective governance system, it impacts all of the other Pastor Factors as well. (See diagram below.) If a pastor has a board who has his back, then he will be freed up to begin changing the church culture to one of equipping rather than doing.

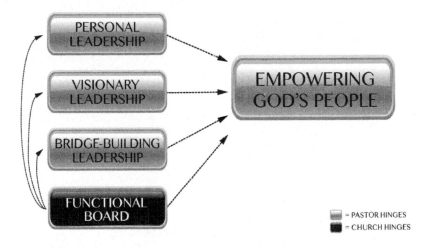

For instance, if a pastor is worried that spending time in the community getting to know and ministering to unreached and lost people will be interpreted as neglecting members, then he will be hesitant to do the "bridge-building" ministry that we mentioned above. The same is true with developing his personal leadership skills or working toward articulating a clear, outward-focused vision to the congregation. On the other hand, if there is a supportive and understanding board approving these actions, then the pastor will have even more freedom to exercise the Empowerment Hinge.

A Functional Board makes a world of difference in helping the pastor implement a culture of empowerment. Rather than siding with those who may complain and whine that the pastor is not "doing" enough, a properly functioning board will protect the pastor who is using his time and effort to equip people for mission and ministry. So when there is a Functional Board, it enables the pastor to do everything better, which in turn makes him even more effective in Empowering God's People.

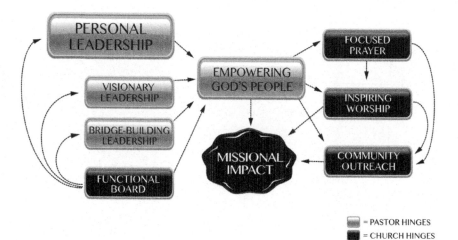

PERSONAL
LEADERSHIP

VISIONARY
LEADERSHIP

BRIDGE-BUILDING
LEADERSHIP

FUNCTIONAL
BOARD

EMPOWERING
GOD'S PEOPLE

FOCUSED
PRAYER

INSPIRING
WORSHIP

COMMUNITY
OUTREACH

MISSIONAL
IMPACT

= PASTOR HINGES
= CHURCH HINGES

5

Personal Leadership

Pastor Mark was "toast." He had just attended his fourth meeting in as many nights. He did not eat well. He was working 80-hour weeks and was worn out. He wondered why he was doing all of this. His leaders seemed apathetic and frustrated, the congregation was restless with his leadership and he hardly got to see his wife and kids.

It hadn't always been that way. Just a couple years earlier, the church was growing, peaking at just over 300 in worship. In 12 years of ministry in a town of 35,000, Pastor Mark had led the congregation from just over 100 to its high point. But it was unravelling, as attendance had dropped to 235, the budget was bleeding red ink and many people were openly disgruntled.

Pastor Mark decided to get some outside help and go through our revitalization process after one of his close friends told him about the turn-around his church had experienced.

Jump ahead two years and Pastor Mark sat at his desk putting the final touches on his remarks for the ordination service for the new associate pastor of the church plant that his congregation started across town. That congregation had grown so rapidly that it already needed a second pastor. He was thankful that God had used him to plant the seeds for that new church and that he still had a close association with this daughter church and its senior pastor.

He was even more grateful that God had completely turned around his own church. What a difference, Pastor Mark thought. Worship attendance had increased to 320, the church budget was in the black, there was a renewed sense of joy on Sunday morning and a strong sense of unity and love among the members and staff. But the best thing was that lives were being changed, both among the members and the many new people to whom the church was ministering from the community.

What Changed?

How were Pastor Mark and his church able to make such dramatic changes in such a short period of time? In this specific situation, the answer is tied to the Hinge of Personal Leadership. Pastor Mark was certainly working hard, much too hard. His long hours and high level of anxiety were taking a huge toll on his health, his marriage, his faith and his career. If he hadn't changed his battle plan, he almost certainly would have been another casualty in the church and ministry wars.

Pastor Mark began to see that in order to lead the church forward, he would have to change himself first. People follow leaders down new paths when those leaders model their own personal change. Robert Quinn, a leadership expert, writes:

> Personal change is a reflection of our inner growth and empower-ment. Empowered leaders … can forcefully communicate at a level beyond telling. By having the courage to change themselves, they model the behavior they are asking of others. Clearly understood by almost everyone, this message, based in integrity, is incredibly powerful. It builds trust and credibility and helps others confront the risk of empowering themselves.[1]

How can a pastor empower and lead the people of his congregation if he isn't able to demonstrate sound leadership in his own life? Pastor Mark was able to change some basic attitudes about the state of the church and his leadership in it. He identified his priorities and began to make space in his life for the things that would allow him to be effective as a leader.

Our research shows that pastors who demonstrate a commitment to their own physical, mental, spiritual and relational needs will be much more effective in empowering their congregations for mission and ministry than those who neglect their own personal development.

People are more willing to exercise spiritual disciplines, if they see their pastor regularly doing those things as well.

Countless times the people of the church have heard preached how they need to share their faith in Jesus with their neighbors, yet little response has resulted. In most cases, it's not because they are unwilling to share their faith, nor do they lack concern for the spiritual condition of their un-churched friends and neighbors. They just don't know what it will look like to overcome their fears about forming relationships with people outside the church and speaking with them about God's love. People follow leaders who are backing up their words with parallel actions, showing them the way. In practical terms, people are more willing to exercise spiritual disciplines like prayer and personal Bible study, engage in community outreach projects and be bold in service and witness, if they see their pastor regularly doing those things as well.

At its core, the Hinge of Personal Leadership is all about modeling, demonstrating to others the way forward. It is instructive that one of the titles our Lord ascribes to himself is "The Way" (John 14:6). He is the only Way to the Father, but he is also the only way period! He is the One to be emulated and followed in all things, including the way that he conducts himself on a daily basis.

As the Apostle Paul succinctly stated, "I urge you to imitate me" (1 Cor. 4:16) i.e., just do what you see me doing. Pretty good advice for pastors—just do what Paul did (and ultimately what Jesus did). And for parishioners—just do what you see your pastor doing … provided that pastor is emulating the One who is the perfect model of Personal Leadership

The Secret of the Big Rocks

The conference presenter filled a big glass pitcher with large rocks. She held it up and asked, "Who thinks this pitcher is full?" A few people raised their hands. Then she took a container of pebbles and poured them in, filling the empty spaces between the rocks. Then she asked, "Now who thinks the pitcher is full?" A few more hands shot up.

Then she poured in some sand. Just like the pebbles previously, the sand filled in the empty spaces around the small rocks. Again she asked, "Who thinks the pitcher is full?" Just about everyone raised their hands.

Finally, she poured a pot of coffee into the pitcher. And just as before, the brown liquid found tiny spaces between the grains of sand.

If you don't put the big rocks in first, you'll never get them in at all.

This illustrates an important lesson about life: If you don't put the big rocks in first, you'll never get them in at all. The Hinge of Personal Leadership is about identifying the big rocks in our lives, our ministry, our faith and our family. If you don't put these big rocks in first, the pebbles, sand and coffee of life will fill up all the space.

Personal Leadership is an exercise in determining what really matters and then making sure you spend an appropriate amount of time in each of those endeavors. For Pastor Mark, it was his family, finishing his ministry well, engaging lost and unreached people with the Gospel and providing quality pastoral care for his church. He came to those conclusions after he and his congregation took the TCN Hinge Assessment Survey.[2] That survey helped him to determine the areas of Personal Leadership where he was strong and where he needed to do more work.

Here are some of the questions contained in the survey:

- Is your pastor deeply committed to his own spiritual growth?
- Does your pastor take care of himself (physically, mentally, etc.)?
- Does your pastor have a healthy, balanced family life?
- Does your pastor use his work time in a disciplined way?
- Does your pastor effectively handle many competing demands on his time?
- Does your pastor intentionally take time to "refresh" outside of church life?
- Is your pastor a man of prayer?
- Does your pastor meet regularly with peers/mentors who keep him spiritually accountable?
- Does your pastor have an open heart to receive counsel from wise, Godly men?

Once Pastor Mark identified the obstacles that were preventing him from reaching his personal and ministry goals, he worked at removing them. Since there were many, he prioritized them according to level of urgency and importance. There were four big rocks that he needed to address, and we have found that these same four are common to most of the pastors we coach. The first we will expound upon at greater length because of the practical challenges and because it impacts the other three.

Big Rock #1: Time Management

Because he felt so harried and burned out, he decided to begin with time management. Of course, for someone who struggles with saying "no" and who has been trained in a culture where the expectation is that you will keep everyone else happy before you tend to your own needs, this is a monumental challenge. Pastor Mark was smart enough to know that he probably wouldn't be able to do this on his own, so he enlisted a coach to help him.[3]

His coach challenged him to understand how he spent his time. One way to do this would be to put together a grid of the major activities that a pastor might find himself doing during any given week. For instance, in the chart in Appendix A entitled "Pastor's Time Log," there are columns for each day of the week. Throughout each day of the week, the pastor notes what he was doing during that particular segment. Then, at the end of the week, he would categorize everything he did into one of the 8 Hinge Factors or 2 Maintenance columns to determine how much time was spent in each general activity.

While there is no perfect template for how the perfect pastor should spend his time each week, there are some general guidelines we find helpful for those who genuinely want to make a missional impact on their community. We summarize the types of work that might fit into each particular category, as well as a suggested amount of time for those activities, found in Appendix A, "Pastor's Time Log."

After a pastor has logged his activities for a few weeks, he will see a pattern emerging that indicates how he uses his time. If he is happy with the division of time among the various categories, no adjustments are needed. However, he may learn that he is spending far too much time doing things he deems to be relatively unimportant, say preparing for meetings or surfing the Internet. And he might discover he is investing very little time in personal Bible study or with his wife and family.

Spiritual leaders need to lead from a well-nourished soul. Leanness of soul can happen all too easily unless leaders find spiritual rhythms that work for them.

The goal of this exercise is to determine what the ideal would look like, especially if the church is to engage its community with the Gospel and make disciples. Some pastors find it helpful to consult with church leaders, as well as family members, to come to a total number of hours and division of categories with which everyone can agree.

This is where the 8 Hinge Factors and Maintenance columns really become helpful. For example, in the case of our imaginary pastor portrayed in Appendix A, there is an inordinately large amount of time spent in

Maintenance. We are not saying that those activities are unimportant. These are just not the activities that are going to lead to growth and disciple-making.

At this point, the pastor can begin to adjust the calendar. It may be as simple as planning blocks of time each week to get into the community for Bridge-Building activities. Or it may be a fundamental shift from primarily caring for the congregation to engaging the community. For instance, if sermon-writing time purposefully includes articulating an outward-focused vision in the message and worship service planning time purposefully includes worship elements that are sensitive to the unchurched, then those activities would shift from the Maintenance column to the Visionary Leadership and Inspiring Worship columns.

Big Rock #2: Personal Health

The next area of concern that Pastor Mark's coach helped him address was his personal health. Since turning fifty, Pastor Mark had noticed that he didn't have the energy he once did, plus he was concerned about the genetic heart disease that ran in his family. He knew that the level of his physical fitness directly impacts the level of energy he has to live the life God is calling him to. Proper diet and exercise patterns become the "gift that keeps on giving."

Some questions to consider in the area of Personal Health and Fitness are:

- What changes do you need to make to increase the amount of energy you need to function well in your ministry and at home?
- What do you need to stop doing or do less of to increase your energy and/or become more healthy?
- What do you need to do to increase the amount of exercise you are getting each week?

Big Rock #3: Spiritual Disciplines

Spiritual leaders need to lead from a well-nourished soul. Leanness of soul can happen all too easily unless leaders find spiritual rhythms that work for them. Every leader needs adequate space in daily life for solitude, reflection, prayer and devotional Bible reading. Pastor Mark knew that in order to lead his congregation into a new era of growth and vitality, he would need to be spiritually strong himself. He also knew how important it would be to model the disciplines necessary to build and maintain that spiritual strength. He found these questions very helpful in putting his plan together for improving his spiritual disciplines:

- When is the best time of the day for you to have personal time with God?
- What usually gets in the way of your time with God?
- What changes would you like to make to reinvigorate your devotional life?

Big Rock #4: Lifelong Learning

Finally, Pastor Mark realized that if he were to sustain this revitalization effort for the long run, he would need to continue to grow and learn. A commitment to lifelong learning is one of the antidotes for overcoming personal plateaus. In today's climate, a leader has a number of outlets for learning, including books, DVDs, podcasts, workshops and conferences.

Some questions you may want to consider as you go about putting together your lifelong learning plan could include:

- What subjects or topics would you like to learn more about?
- What area of life or ministry do you need to learn more about?
- When is the best time of the week for you to dedicate time to this kind of learning?

Personal Retreat: A Great Way to Prioritize the Big Rocks

During the first few weeks after Pastor Mark put his plan into action, he did relatively well. However, over time, his resolve began to waver. He found himself reverting back to old habits. Fearing that all his work would be undone, he asked his coach for advice. Basing his counsel on the practice of Jesus, his coach suggested going away on a monthly personal retreat.

And when evening had come, after the sun had set, they began bringing to him all who were ill and those who were demon-possessed. And the whole city had gathered at the door. And he healed many who were ill with various diseases, and cast out many demons; and he was not permitting the demons to speak, because they knew who he was. And in the early morning, while it was still dark, he arose and went out and departed to a lonely place, and was praying there. And Simon his companion hunted for him; and they found him and said to him, "Everyone is looking for You." And he said to them," Let us go somewhere else to the towns nearby, in order that I may preach there also; for that is what I came out for" (Mark 1:32-38).

Leaders are set apart as they see what no one else does, developing an ability to have bifocal vision, the ability to see both the immediate needs along with that which is distant. However, like Jesus experienced, the whole city is at the door. Today's church leaders face incredible demands. Legitimate and urgent needs come from every direction.

Jesus must have been exhausted after ministering to the needs we see in Mark 1. Thereafter, he departed and went out to a lonely place, and something wonderful happened for him. Vitality, perspective, strength and a reconnection with the call that was on His life all began to seep back into His soul. So much so that he confounded his disciples by telling them that he

Leaders are set apart as they see what no one else does, developing an ability to have bifocal vision.

needed to move on to another town. Other people's agendas did not dictate what Jesus was going to give His life to.

While a personal retreat is not a panacea for all that ails a pastor, it can make the space in your life for personal reflection about big rocks. God has invaluable treasures awaiting the leader who regularly withdraws from the battlefront to replenish and refocus his life. Many leaders find that a monthly day away has become the cornerstone of their effectiveness and vitality. Withdrawing has become for them the most important day of the month. Let's be honest though, ministry is often an adrenaline rush. We go from one meeting to the next, from one project to another, from one deep need to an even deeper need. Everything around you, "the city at the door," will tell you that you cannot withdraw. The enemy of our souls knows that life change is awaiting you at the summit where you meet with God and he shows you the next steps for the journey.

A Hero's Journey

As Pastor Mark prioritized his big rocks, he found that there were some deep things within him that the Lord wanted to change. During his time of working 80-hour weeks, he had taken on the defeatist attitudes of angry church members who were expressing their helplessness about the struggles of the church. Now, Pastor Mark had learned to regard the present realities as opportunities. These opportunities called for spiritual warfare, in which pastor and people would need to pray more fervently than ever against the oppression they had been experiencing and depend on the Lord to lead them into this brave new frontier. This is leadership shaped by the image of "hero's journey," which is simply ...

... a story of individual transformation, a change of identity. In embarking on the journey, we must leave the world of certainty. We must courageously journey to a strange place where there are a lot of risks and much is at stake, a place where there are new problems that require us to think in new ways. Because there is much at stake, we must engage and resolve the problems before us. To do this successfully, we must surrender our present self—we must step outside our old paradigms.[4]

Considering himself on a "hero's journey," instead of a fool's errand, gave new energy to Pastor Mark. This journey involved meeting and relating to people outside the church, as we will see in the chapter on Building Bridges. But the personal change he experienced provided him with courage to lead the congregation to a new place and in new ways.

> **Personal Leadership is about developing the courage and disciplines required to lead others through open doors and into the community.**

When Pastor Mark embarked on his "hero's journey," it was accompanied by a deeper dependence on the Lord than he had experienced in some years. As he examined and reset priorities and paid more attention to his own physical and spiritual well-being, he began to exude a confident and optimistic spirit which had an uplifting effect on the church members.

Personal Leadership is about developing the courage and disciplines required to lead others through open doors and into the community. It's about the deep personal change that allows a leader to adapt to new and challenging circumstances. Behaviors that embrace the new and uncharted territory as an opportunity rather than obstacle will refresh and inspire the members as they see their pastor walk through the open doors of the church and lead with courage and discipline.

Discussion Questions

1. What are the "big rocks" in your life? Give examples where the pebbles, sand and coffee of life may be taking up too much space in your pitcher.

2. Apply the "Hinge Assessment Survey" questions from page 60 to your situation, i.e., substitute your own name for the position of "your pastor." How would you rate yourself overall in the Hinge of Personal Leadership? In what areas would you like to improve? What obstacles need to be removed?

3. Of the four big rocks named in the chapter (Time Management, Personal Health, Spiritual Discipline, and Lifelong Learning), which one do you struggle with the most? What could you do to change that?

4. Read Mark 1:32-38. How have you experienced "the whole city ... at your door" or being "hunted" lately? What seemed to happen for Jesus when he departed to a lonely place? How do you think Simon and the others responded to Jesus' reply in verse 38? What are you personally challenged by in this passage?

5. If you were to embark on a "hero's journey" in the next few months, where would the journey take you? Who would go with you?

PERSONAL
LEADERSHIP

VISIONARY
LEADERSHIP

BRIDGE-BUILDING
LEADERSHIP

FUNCTIONAL
BOARD

EMPOWERING
GOD'S PEOPLE

FOCUSED
PRAYER

INSPIRING
WORSHIP

COMMUNITY
OUTREACH

MISSIONAL
IMPACT

= PASTOR HINGES
= CHURCH HINGES

6

Visionary Leadership

You have saved up your money, coordinated your vacation days with the kids' school break, studied the brochures, bought the tickets, reserved hotel rooms—and now you and your family are off to Disney World. This trip did not just appear on the horizon like today's weather; it was the anticipated culmination of plans and activities. It will be expensive, requiring some sacrifices on the part of each member of the family, so you won't be able to afford the very best hotel or get to see every attraction. There will be differences of opinion as to which attractions to visit, and some compromise and concessions will be required.

Before any plans were made, there was a vision: we are going to Disney World! This singular vision was one the entire family could get behind. Dad could see himself behind the camera as the kids engaged Mickey. Jenny imagined herself going 'round and 'round in giant revolving teacups, while Bret set his sights on more dignified pursuits at Epcot. Mom was setting aside funds for some break-away time to do some serious shopping. The details of the hoped-for experience were diverse, but the vision was clear.

Churches also have visions of where they are going. Like the Orlando-bound family, the trip should be exciting and have goals for the greater good of all who are involved. Likewise, it will call for careful planning and budgeting along with compromise and alignment of values. But the vision ties it all together.

What is Vision?

Stated simply, vision is "a clear picture of a preferred future." Most churches, however, like most people, think of vision in a general way—doing good things, carrying out good activities, fulfilling the general mandates of the Bible. They see the big biblical principles or purposes of the church and try to move in that direction. The problem, however, is that those principles and purposes are so broad that it is impossible to accomplish all of them, let alone measure if you are actually hitting any of those broad targets. Like the common saying about hunting goes, "Aim at everything and you will hit nothing!"

Most churches, however, like most people, think of vision in a general way— doing good things, carrying out good activities, fulfilling the general mandates of the Bible.

The Hinge Factor of Visionary Leadership points to a very specific future direction and target(s) for the local church. In our research, we found that when there is a clear and specific vision, the pastor is freed up to focus on the central Hinge Factor of Empowering God's People, resulting in a greater missional impact.

Every church has a vision, an idea about where it is going. For some the vision is vague, perhaps lacking in enough specificity for anything to be done about it. For others, the vision may be too scattered, involving more targets than anyone in the church has energy to pursue. Some church visions are wishful thoughts about a brighter future; others are pessimistic pictures of the inevitable demise of the institution. Some churches have made attempts at written vision statements, while most have unstated default visions of just doing what has always been done.

While pastoring, a young African-American woman visited my (David's) church. In spite of the multicultural community in which we were located, our congregation was almost entirely composed of older white people of Germanic descent. As I greeted her after the service, she expressed that she had gotten a lot out of the worship and was really glad that she had come. "But ..." she started to say, and then looked away. "But you won't be back because you are the only black person here?" I said. "Yes, that's it," she said with an awkward smile. "And if you don't come back, we will never change," I replied.

At that point, I briefly shared our vision to engage our community in spite of what we looked like on Sunday mornings. This glimpse into our future gave her enough that she did return and join us. Ten years later, the English-speaking congregation consisted of people from 30 different ethnic and national backgrounds, and there were five new culture-specific daughter congregations worshiping Jesus in our facility. This new life arose because we had a new vision.

What Vision Produces

Church consultant George Bullard, in his thesis *The Life Cycle and Stages of Congregational Development,*[1] explains how the life of a church and the vision that drives it works. He simply recognized that churches are much like people. They are born, they grow up and eventually they die. (See diagram on the next page.) The only difference is that people only get one life, while churches can have multiple life cycles.

The life cycle of a church organization can be graphed as a bell-shaped curve starting with birth, growing toward maturity and declining through retirement to eventual death. Like people, a church's life cycle typically takes place over a period of 75-100 years. Some congregations close earlier and a few may have exceptionally good genes for longevity, but no congregation lasts forever, unless it starts a new life cycle. In the history of the church, countless new life cycles have spun off, beginning with the early churches that we read about in Acts, and now

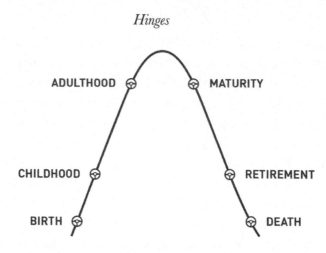

most churches find themselves in a place where they can either continue down the slope of decline or launch forward into a new life cycle.

Seeing the normal development of a church's life cycle can be freeing. Because it is a natural process for an organization, just like that of human aging, it can help a church see that the current state of decline is not an abnormal experience or something that requires us to find someone to blame. At the same time, even though getting older is unavoidable, we are not happy about it either. Likewise, the decline of church organizations, while normal and expected, creates a discomfort and sense of urgency that drives congregations to ask, "How do we start a new life cycle?"

The earlier a new life cycle gets started the better the chances are for its success. In other words, the longer a church waits once it starts progressing along the slope of decline, the harder it is to launch a new life cycle. Unfortunately, congregations in the early part of their decline usually deny their situation and will not see the need for starting a new life cycle until much later when there are too few people with too little energy and too few resources to readily make it happen. The key to starting a new life cycle, then, is proactivity, and this proactivity is tied to vision.

The earlier a new life cycle gets started the better the chances are for its success.

In Bullard's model, there are four components that shape a life cycle: Vision, Relationships, Ministries, and Structure. Vision gets at the heart of a congregation's purpose and

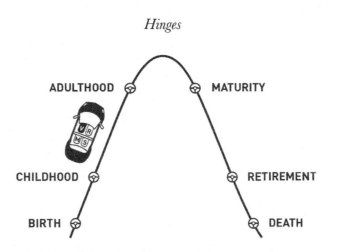

ADULTHOOD   MATURITY

CHILDHOOD   RETIREMENT

BIRTH   DEATH

keeps our eyes focused on where we are going.

Relationships are the arms that embrace the people, especially new people, who will carry out the vision. Ministries are the hands that do the work that support the vision, and Structure is the skeleton, which gives form and organization to the process and holds everyone accountable for carrying out the vision.

A new life cycle is driven by Vision and Relationships. For instance, in the diagram above, we see an aerial sketch of an automobile ascending the life cycle from birth toward maturity.

Vision is in the driver's seat with Relationships riding "shotgun" in the front passenger seat. Ministry and Structure are riding in the back seat of the car as it ascends the life-cycle curve toward maturity. This does not mean that these two components are less important than Vision and Relationships; it only means that they play a supportive role.

By contrast, a church that is in decline exhibits a different configuration of riders in the car. In the diagram on the next page, the automobile heading down from maturity through the stages of decline finds Structure behind the wheel. The Structure morphs from a supportive player to a heartless dictator, which focuses on itself. Typically, we will see a handful of people that remain as members of a church desperately trying to cobble together enough officers to fill all the various positions demanded by the constitution, often forcing individuals to take on multiple hats.

Ministry programs ride along next to Structure in the "crash" seat as the car accelerates down the backside of the life cycle. We do what

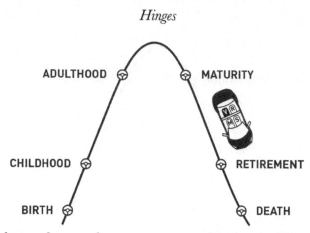

we have always done as long as we can without pausing to ask why. Can we still keep a choir going, even if our voices are weaker and there are too few of us to sing in parts? And maybe we should find a young person to lead a youth group—after all, the youth are the future of our church, you know.

This picture of a dying church where Structure dictates and Ministries are ends-in-themselves need not be the case for your church. A clear vision of a preferred future can move back into the driver's seat and move the church into a new life cycle.

Paint a Picture of the Future

Vision opens the door to the new possibility of a new future, a new life cycle for the church, as illustrated on the next page. It reveals who you are and where you are going. Vision impacts the values, character and activities of a congregation. Amongst the complexity of a church organization, composed of many different people doing all kinds of different things, vision is the one overarching rallying point. Vision is what we see the congregation looking like in a future preferred by all, whereby each participant can see themselves in an exciting, or at least satisfying, place in that future. Whether riding the teacups or browsing the shops or revitalizing a church, it all is possible in the preferred future, and we are all motivated to work and even sacrifice to get there.

There are two foci around which the vision will develop: inward

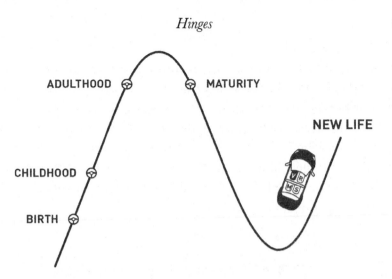

and outward. When I (David) was a parish pastor, I failed to call on a long-term member who was in the hospital. While the news of this person's hospitalization did not reach me, the news of my apparent neglect quickly spread throughout the congregation. Clearly there were expectations of the pastor's role that were non-negotiable, and I heard about it. At the same time, there were thousands of unchurched people in the community who were dying spiritually and did not have my attention or the attention of the church, but nobody complained about that. For the most part, we did not think about the unchurched people and their needs because they were not knocking on the church door asking, "When are you going to get around to telling us about Jesus?"

The vision must recognize the need for balance between both the inward and outward dimensions of church life. At the same time, since most organizations tend to be self-serving, it is crucial that the vision focus outward. God has a mission for "all to be saved and come to a knowledge of the truth" (1 Timothy 2:4) and for the church to participate in the God-given commission to "make disciples of all nations" (Matt. 28:19).

Vision is what we see the congregation looking like in a future preferred by all, whereby each participant can see themselves in an exciting, or at least satisfying, place in that future.

The vision of a new life cycle will place a heavier emphasis on the outward component, because the unchurched do not speak for themselves and can easily be invisible to the people of the church. Accordingly, our bias is to encourage congregations to focus on missional targets, because the assumption is that the inward components are already essentially provided for. It is not improper, nevertheless, to include some inward targets in a vision statement, especially as they relate to strengthening the members in their faith so that they might more effectively serve the Great Commission.

Writing a Compelling Vision Statement

A compelling vision statement:

- Describes a preferable future. Think of vision as a snapshot of a congregation three to five years from now. What things would be taking place that are not happening now? Like a photograph, the vision statement will include all kinds of details as well as give an overall impression of what the congregation will look like. This is not a picture of lots of smiling faces attending church services, but a picture of members serving in the community, interacting with new people and sharing the Gospel while they share themselves with those around them. What places in the community would be in that picture? What people groups would be there? What kinds of specific needs would be met?
- Has an emotional impact. Andy Stanley in his book *Visioneering* writes, "Visions are born in the soul of a man or woman who is consumed with the tension between what is and what could be."[2] Vision taps into the passion of people who are not satisfied with things as they are. They are not content to sum up their commitment to Jesus and His Word in a weekly one-hour worship service. They are not fulfilled by a church that prides itself on being well-organized or friendly to each other, while so many people all around it have not heard the good news of salvation in Jesus. Vi-

sion generally starts with a pastor and a small group of passionate people who will not settle for a church that is focused on itself, its past or its survival.

- Has specificity. People often confuse vision statements with mission statements, assuming that they are synonymous. The vision statement lays out some specifics that flesh out the missional values of the congregation. For instance, the vision statement of a particular congregation may identify "families with young children" as one of its critical targets, and that may be a logical choice if the church already operates a preschool. The statement could envision specific needs of young families in the community being met by the congregation's ministry, but it would not necessarily need to lay out the specifics of parenting seminars, support groups, children's ministry programs and the like.

Vision generally starts with a pastor and a small group of passionate people who will not settle for a church that is focused on itself.

- Is memorable, but not memorized. After all the possible mission targets are laid out, they should be narrowed down to four or fewer. Energy and resources will rapidly dissipate where there are too many critical targets. Most commonly, congregations identify three critical mission targets. Larger churches may select more, and smaller churches should select fewer. Once three or four critical targets are established, each will form a section of the vision statement, so that while no one will be memorizing the statement, everyone will be able to recount the three or four targets that form the basis of their vision.

- Lasts three to five years. It works best to think about the vision in terms of three to five years. Most congregations can see themselves surviving for the next five years, so working through a process in which there is a high probability of positive results in that time frame makes sense. A three- to five-year vision is not forever, but it is long enough to accomplish something when everyone in the organization is committed to it.

Now let's look at vision development in two specific churches. The first example is the story of a church which had only recently begun its downward journey in its life cycle. They did not wait until the situation became obviously painful to talk about vision. The church in the second example, on the other hand, was nearing death before they realized that they needed a new vision.

Visioning at the Point of "Maturity"

Redeemer is a congregation of moderate size located in the exurbs of a large metropolitan area. Her pastor of many years was a visionary leader who steadfastly kept the focus of the ministry on mission from the beginning of his tenure. Despite this, the secularization of post-modern Western society had taken a toll on Redeemer, to the point that in 2010 it did not have the same vitality as it once had. It had moved over the hump of the life cycle into the stage of "maturity."

Even though they were not experiencing obvious decline, the pastor wanted to set the church up for a new life cycle of ministry to their community before he retired in a few years. He began by organizing prayer-walking events around town. This stretched members beyond their comfort zones as they related to people in their community. While walking around town, the members offered to pray for people's needs, and most people whom they approached were open to it. They were most surprised by the positive response by shopkeepers who welcomed prayer in difficult economic times. The faith of one businessman was renewed, and he invited the people of Redeemer to begin a house church right in his store.

A visioning task force consisting of the pastor and a few leaders was designated to work through the demographics and community surveys in preparation for the Visioning Day.[3] On the Day of Visioning, the ministry to shopkeepers was one of many candidates for mission targets up for discussion. The vision question for Redeemer was not "what can we do?" but rather "what should we do first, and with which mission target can we do the best job?" By the end of that day, it was clear that most of the targets that surfaced could be organized under three general categories. It was then the job of the visioning task force to put them into a draft vision statement.

The final vision statement approved by the members of Redeemer had three general categories, and it had a list of specific initiatives with goals and strategies in each category. The pastor kept the vision before the congregation in sermons and publications of the church, and the board began to reorganize the congregation's decision-making process around the vision. Because the goals and strategies were spelled out with specificity, it was not difficult for the congregation to begin living out their new vision.

A few years later when the pastor retired, the process of calling the next pastor was informed by this new outward-focused vision. In the call process, the congregation was able to state where it believed God was leading them and then ask how this might coincide with the vision of the pastoral candidate. Calling a pastor on the basis of visionary leadership has a distinct advantage over calling a pastor on the basis of his preaching, record of caregiving or where he originally came from. Asking what the vision of the new pastor is, and if that vision is compatible with that of the congregation, is a much better question.

Visioning in a Declining Congregation

While Redeemer was not descending down the back half of its life cycle in obvious ways, this was not the case for Trinity. Located in a first-tier suburb that developed in the late 1940s, it was progressing quickly from the "retirement" stage to "death." After growing rapidly through the 1950s and 1960s with a peak membership of 600, it began to decline. Its founding vision to serve a growing community of post-World War II families included the building of a large facility tailored to the needs of young families at the time. Beginning in the 1970s, the vision grew stale as the population aged and shifted. The founding pastor retired and the congregation called a new pastor who was skilled at pastoral care and preaching. By the 2000s, Trinity found itself in full survival mode with fewer than 50 people attending services on an average Sunday.

In desperation they engaged our assistance, hoping for the proverbial silver bullet. They eagerly embraced the idea of a new vision for the future, but initially allowed their wishful thinking to trump the realities. They approached the visioning process by dreaming of a future where the pews were full of young people who were stuffing large sums of money into the offering plates.

We kept stressing that God's vision for the church is to seek and to save the lost (Luke 19:9) and that if we seek to build the Kingdom of God as a first priority, then "all these things will be added also" (Matthew 6:33). Gradually the people of Trinity rediscovered their missional purpose as we encouraged them to pray consistently for an outward-focused vision and for unbelieving and unchurched people that they knew in their community.

In their demographic survey, they discovered that their community had many young families and that a large number of immigrants from south Asia had moved into their area.

At the Visioning Day, after hours of prayer and discussion, the Holy Spirit sovereignly moved among them, and unanimity emerged around three areas of vision. First, Trinity saw themselves in the next three to five years ministering to families with young children. This was a good place to start because Trinity already ran a moderately successful preschool. By making the unchurched families of their preschool a mission target, the congregation realized that they needed to stop regarding it as a source of income for the church and start spending some of their resources to improve the quality of the preschool. They also developed strategies to help the church members form personal relationships with the preschool families.

The second mission target was to discover and meet some of the needs of the growing immigrant population. This was a taller order because there were no members of this people group represented in the church, and no one had any idea of how to build bridges into this community. The people of Trinity nonetheless felt that there were too many new neighbors to ignore and envisioned themselves having something to do with this population.

This led to the third mission target: Trinity would look for creative partnerships to help them address the other two. With little energy and few resources, Trinity realized that it would take some outside help to start a new life cycle.

It wasn't long before God began answering their prayers. A young bi-cultural pastor in their area had started a number of house churches, and they had grown to the point where they were looking for a worship facility. He began meeting with his new multicultural church at Trinity, and a partnership ensued that served everyone's needs. At Trinity, the pastor found the loving support and the denominational home he had been looking for. Before long, he was serving as the pastor of both churches, and they were on the way to becoming one church which had something to offer everybody that lived in that community.

If this was not miraculous enough, the pastor's wife was an experienced preschool administrator who helped improve the quality of Trinity's preschool and its potential as a mission outpost in the community.

Of course, there is no way to predict the emergence of new partners to assist a congregation, but this is where faith comes in. Some might view the advent of this young pastor and his house churches as a happy coincidence, but the people of Trinity regarded it as nothing short of a miraculous answer to prayer. Like so many of God's gifts, they become available to us as we shed our pride, assert our dependence on him and prayerfully open ourselves to new things.

Leading into the Future

If your family wants to go to Disney World, it starts with a vision. There are no teacups and pictures with Mickey without a compelling picture that invites the entire family to contribute to the journey. Without this, the family experience will remain the same, never going beyond what it already knows.

Your church has the opportunity to be far more than what it has been in the past. It can do more than survive. It can be a light to the community, a source of life to the dying. When you catch God's picture of what you can be, only God knows the ways that you will be used to touch others.

Discussion Questions

1. What is the current vision of your church? (If you are discussing these questions in a group, silently write a sentence or two describing how you see your church's vision before comparing your description with the whole group.) How closely does your perception of the church's vision match the perception of others?

2. How are the life cycles of churches and people similar? How are they different? How are the four components of a life cycle configured in a church going up the life cycle? Going down the life cycle?

3. Where would you say your church is on the life cycle right now? Why? Which components are in the front seat and which ones are in the back seat? Give examples.

4. If your church is on the down side of the life cycle (or is plateaued), what do you think needs to happen to start a new life cycle? If it is on the up side, what do you think needs to happen to sustain the current path?

5. Activity for next week:

    By yourself or in a group, do a brief survey of your community. You can approach people in your own neighborhood, go to a mall, park or other public place or even knock on doors if you feel really bold. Begin by briefly identifying yourself, saying "I'm a member of _____ Church, and I'm doing a short three question survey. Do you have a minute to answer three questions?"

    1. What three words would you use to describe _____ Church?
    2. What needs do you see people in our community struggle with meeting?

3. If you were looking for a church home, what characteristics or qualities would you look for?

Be sure to jot down a few notes on their answers, thank them and if you feel comfortable, ask, "Would you have any needs or requests that we might pray for?" Then just be on your way.

PERSONAL LEADERSHIP

VISIONARY LEADERSHIP

BRIDGE-BUILDING LEADERSHIP

FUNCTIONAL BOARD

EMPOWERING GOD'S PEOPLE

FOCUSED PRAYER

INSPIRING WORSHIP

COMMUNITY OUTREACH

MISSIONAL IMPACT

= PASTOR HINGES
= CHURCH HINGES

7

Bridge-Building Leadership

A congregation in a mid-sized city in Florida wanted to know what the average person in their city thought of their church. They sent out teams to interview 300 people at malls, in parks and in other public places. They began the interviews by asking for three words to describe their church. The responses were surprisingly similar as most people stated that they had never heard of the church. After the interviewers described the church with the fountain on its front lawn, the majority said they thought the building was a bank.

The fact that few in the community knew that it was a church was eye-opening for this congregation. Even though they had good signage, a building that looked like a lot of other church buildings and a name that was clearly Christian, the average person in their city had no knowledge, much less an opinion, about what the church was up to.

This experience opened their eyes to their post-church culture. The average non-churchgoer is not paying much attention to what goes on in church buildings. They are not looking to the church to provide spiritual answers to life's problems. Think about the visitors and new members who have joined your church in the last year. How many of them had an unchurched background? When we ask this of church leaders in seminars, pastors confess that almost all the new people who join their churches are Christians who have quit attending previous churches and are now looking for something else.

To reach our world with the Gospel, we must open the door outward so that we can build bridges to our communities, to meet people where they live, play and work.

The doors of our churches open inward. To reach our world with the Gospel, we must open the door outward so that we can build bridges to our communities, to meet people where they live, play and work. We must go to them instead of expecting them to come to us. Jesus himself said, "Therefore, go into all the world and make disciples." He didn't say, "Just sit back and wait for people to come to you!"

Opening the doors of the church involves the work of the pastor as a bridge builder to the community. He models the relational work of connecting with people so that others will follow him out the door and over the bridge into the community. The leadership of the pastor is key to this because he is the scout or vanguard of the church reaching into the community. When pastors build effective bridges, this activity directly impacts a congregation's ability to Empower God's People to pray, worship and engage in Community Outreach, which in turn has a missional impact on the community.

What Really Matters

Studies have been performed through the years evaluating how pastors spend their time and invest their energy. These studies often break pastors' time commitments into four categories:

1. Reading, Studying and Sermon Preparation
2. Counseling, Regular Visitation to Members, Hospitals and Shut-ins

3. Administration, Church Committees, Other Meetings and Budget Concerns

4. Doing Personal Evangelism and Training Others to Do It

Understanding the way that pastors spend their time is revealing. For the pastors in the first category—Reading, Studying and Sermon Preparation—their churches remain comprised of the same people, just older, with some transfer growth from other churches.

The results found about those in the second group who focus on Counseling, Regular Visitation to Members, Hospitals and Shut-ins, are similar to those in the first, however, the transfer growth is lower because of the focus on caring for existing members.

The pastors from the third category who invest their efforts on Administration, Church Committees, Other Meetings and Budget Concerns see a sharp decrease in the number and attendance of the members, very few transfers and survival becomes the chief aim of the pastor and leaders.

In contrast to the first three, the fourth group of churches, where the pastor emphasizes Doing Personal Evangelism and Training Others to Do the Same sees dramatically different results. In these churches, where there is considerable time devoted by the pastor to build bridges into the community as he forms relationships with individuals and groups in order to share the Gospel with them and thereby modeling for and training his members to do the same, there are some amazing results. There is an increase in new people coming into the church, both among transfers and previously non-churched or unbelieving people, the existing members are energized and attend worship services more often, and the pastor himself becomes more focused on the future growth of the church. Perhaps best of all, much of the increase comes from younger people who are now being reached.

The growth of the church is not dependent on the initial size of the church, its location, its socioeconomic situation or its style of ministry. What is abundantly clear, however, is that pastors can dramatically affect the growth of their church by focusing on what really matters, that is what we call bridge building.

The Pastor's Two-fold Role in Bridge Building:
Scout and Model

In the beginning, God created heaven and earth and communed with Adam, whom he created in his own image. However, because of disobedience and pride, sin came into the world, creating a gulf between God and man. In vain, man has tried to reach across the gulf, but it was just not possible. God alone was able to bridge the gap, but at great cost—the life of His Son. He sent His Son into the world by becoming incarnate to pay the price for sin and bridge the gap between us.

Part of the word "incarnation" includes the Latin word *carne*, which means flesh. In Jesus' birth God came "into the flesh." "The Word became flesh and dwelt among us" (John 1:14). God, in Christ, became a human being, so he could relate to us and build a bridge between himself and us. The incarnate Christ entered into our everyday life, showing us the way to eternal peace with the Father and modeling what it looks like to have a loving relationship with other people.

The task of the bridge-builder is essential to effective leadership. In ancient Rome, one of the titles of the Emperor was *Pontifex Maximus*, which translates as "The Greatest Builder of Bridges." Because Rome was a conglomeration of disparate cultures, the Emperor had to relate to these diverse people. Later, the Pope took on this same title as he also had to bridge many lands and cultures. While modesty should prevent a

The incarnate Christ entered into our everyday life, showing us the way to eternal peace with the Father and modeling what it looks like to have a loving relationship with other people.

modern-day pastor from thinking of himself as an Emperor or a Pope, as head of his church organization he is nonetheless first and foremost a bridge-builder. This work is carried out in two ways: scouting and modeling.

First, let's consider the role of the scout as illustrated in the Exodus story. Within two years of leaving Egyptian bondage under Moses' leadership, the children of Israel were on the threshold of the Promised Land at Kadesh-Barnea. Moses sent a member of each tribe ahead into the Promised Land as scouts to see what the land was like as well as to understand its challenges. Based on their reconnaissance, plans and strategies could be established back in the camp. Like all scouts, they came back with "some good news and some bad news." Caleb and Joshua encouraged the people with talk of "milk and honey," but grimmer news from the other scouts about the warring tribes of giants gave the people cold feet. They chose to ignore the encouragement of their leaders that the Spirit of God would empower them and wound up wandering back in the wilderness for another thirty-eight years.

The pastor builds bridges into the community and walks over them to scout out the territory. Who lives there, what they are like, what they need, what they have in common with us, what challenges will present themselves in regard to relating to them—these are all part of the data the pastor brings back with him to encourage and equip his members for the adventure. The reaction on the home front can be mixed, as it was in Moses' day: some will be ready for the challenge while others will want to retreat deep within the church and close the doors. The implementation of the vision to make disciples in the world around the church will rise or fall on the passion and preparedness of the members under the pastor's leadership, or the lack thereof.

The other aspect of the Bridge-Building which falls at first on the pastor is modeling. When I (David) began to delegate the work of pastoral care in my parish to my elders, their blood ran cold. It was not long, however, after taking them out on shut-in calls and hospital visits that they were doing this on their own. They watched what I did at first and were encouraged to incrementally do the same things on subsequent visits. It worked the same way with street ministry. I was scared stiff to attempt this, but I prayed for courage and forced myself to go out into the streets of my urban neighborhood and offer gospel tracts to strangers, seeking to engage them in conversations. Having survived a few rounds of this activity, I equipped and encouraged some of my bolder members to join me, and soon they were ministering two-by-two on street corners all over our neighborhood.

What Jesus Modeled

The Gospels reveal that Jesus focused a huge part of his ministry on empowering key leaders. To fully understand what he passed to the disciples, we must look beyond what he taught to the ways that Jesus ministered. One of the best illustrations of this is found in Luke 19:

When Jesus reached the spot, he looked up and said to him, "Zacchaeus, come down immediately. I must stay at your house today." So he came down at once and welcomed him gladly. All the people saw this and began to mutter, "He has gone to be the guest of a 'sinner.'" But Zacchaeus stood up and said to the Lord, "Look, Lord! Here and now I give half of my possessions to the poor, and if I have cheated anybody out of anything, I will pay back four times the amount." Jesus said to him, "Today salvation has come to this house, because this man, too, is a son of Abraham" (Luke 19:5-9).

Jesus was merely passing through the city that day. Zacchaeus was not necessarily on His ministry agenda, but he went out of his way to Zacchaeus' home, even staying with him. Jesus' life-style was such that he was always looking for lost people and was ready to shift his schedule when the opportunity presented itself. Jesus noticed seekers. He started the conversation (as he did with the woman in John 4) not waiting for someone else to set the stage. While many lost people behave in ways that cause some Christians to exclude them, Jesus was not afraid to associate with those labeled as "sinners" or afraid of what others would think of him.

What Pastors Model

Any pastor can tell his members that they need to get out into the community and make relationships with unchurched people, but they won't know how to do this unless someone shows them. Pastor Paul agreed, but he knew that this would be a shift for him. While serving a congregation in a small town in the upper Midwest, his ministry coach encouraged him to spend eight hours per week in the community outside of the church building. This came as a shock, as he was rather shy and withdrawn by nature. While he did an excellent job caring for his flock, was a polished public speaker and ran a well-organized ministry, when it came to conversations with strangers, he was petrified.

Many pastors with whom we work share Pastor Paul's sentiments. Some are introverts according to their personality, while others have just worked with people they know inside the church for so long that they have not developed their bridge-building muscles. It's nearly impossible to change your nature if you are shy, retiring and conflict averse among people you don't know very well. However, many leaders have become effective bridge-builders in spite of their tendencies.

The key is to begin developing some bridge-building muscles by adopting some basic exercises. Here are three. First, pray. Ask the Lord to give you boldness that arises out of love for people. And pray for individuals. The more you pray for someone, the more you will see that person with the eyes of the Spirit of God.

Secondly, step out and talk to people. For those who don't naturally connect with those they don't know, this is the biggest hurdle. After the ice is broken and some common ground established, conversations come naturally. But you have to initiate the conversation.

One pastor who is shy by nature shared how he began exercising his bridge-building muscles by doing something different. He sat at a table with a family he didn't know at a church picnic. The people at the table were talking to each other, but not to him. "They probably resent me crashing their table," he thought to himself. Then

> **The more you pray for someone, the more you will see that person with the eyes of the Spirit of God.**

he wondered, "What if they're like me, and they don't want to take the risk either." When he overheard them talking about taking a trip to Italy, he asked, "Where in Italy did you go?" They were glad to talk about their trip, and a conversation ensued. He soon learned that the woman shared the same hobby as his wife, which led to an ongoing connection around that hobby over the next few weeks. The connection was natural, after he stepped out and began the conversation.

The third exercise is to partner with some people who are more outgoing in nature, those who naturally strike up conversations and network with others. Gene is so gregarious that some think he is flighty, but he makes everybody feel at home. At coffee hour after church he finds the newcomers who are standing alone and engages them in conversation. Usually he asks them questions about themselves, and that gets the ball rolling. He met Al in this setting and found out he grew up in Ohio. Immediately he led him over to John, a native of Ohio, and introduced them. After he got Al and John talking about Ohio, he moved on to start another conversation.

Pastor Paul, who was making his peace with the challenging advice of his coach, depended upon Gene to work the room in every gathering, and it always produced new relationships. After Pastor Paul started spending significant periods of time in the community, he decided to move his office into the coffee shop on Main Street. They had free WI-FI, and he could do his work when the shop was empty. When people came and sat nearby, he would break the ice and ask some pleasant non-threatening questions. In addition, he would often have his meetings there, specifically with Gene. Conversations on those days were especially easy. They discovered needs about which they prayed. At one point, Pastor Paul shared his faith with the barista.

In the next chapter, we will discuss an intentional way to take this experience to the next level through Triads. This essentially involves three people meeting in a public place like a coffee shop and having a faith conversation that others might overhear and join. That would be a next step for Pastor Paul and hopefully Gene could help with getting that started.

Making Room for New Relationships

Pastors and people extending themselves to be in places where they can meet new people and be intentional about engaging them and relating to them all takes time and emotional energy. However, most Pastors don't have much extra time and energy. People are like Legos, children's building blocks that each have eight connectors.

Sociologists tell us most people have the capacity to have about eight close friends. Most people in our churches have all of their connectors filled up with other church members, so there isn't room to add anyone new. And most pastors have all of their connectors filled up—and sometimes over filled—with connections to church members.

Most people in our churches have all of their connectors filled up with other church members, so there isn't room to add anyone new.

The trick is to free up some space on our Legos for new people. There are really only a couple of ways to do that. One is by being less involved with church duties or other life activities. (See Chapter 4 on Empowering God's People for some practical steps.) The other is by intentionally spending less time with our current friends from church and more time developing relationships with those outside the church.

As you rethink how your Lego connectors are filled, the next question you face is How do you find these new people? Where do you find folks who don't have a relationship with Jesus Christ, and how do you begin to build a truly meaningful relationship with them?

Third Places

Pastor Paul came to realize that because it was difficult for him to meet and relate to new people, he needed to find a setting more conducive for bridging into the community than his church office. What he found in the coffee shop was a typical "Third Place." This concept is based on the premise that there are three places where most of us spend the bulk of our time. The first place is our home, the place where we belong just because we are who we are.

The second is the place of work, or school for students. It's where you are accepted conditionally, based on what you do and whether or not you fit in with a particular group or culture.

Third places are simply places where people connect with others outside the home and work. The old sitcom *Cheers* illustrates this. It's the place where "everybody knows your name." Here, people don't come because they must but because they want to. They come to converse, usually in a light-hearted manner with others who are "regulars." In some ways, this place provides a home away from home.

Examples of third places include coffee shops and cafes, bars and pubs, restaurants, community centers, senior centers, stores, malls, markets, hair salons, barber shops, recreation centers, YM/WCA, pools, movie theaters, libraries and parks. Here people find connections, conversation partners and explore ideas. They come and go as they like and the pressure from expectations is low.

Identify the third places in your community. Where are the coffee shops, the restaurants, the bars, the places where people hang out? Begin to frequent one or two of them. Get to know the patrons. Befriend the proprietors.

It's All About Relationships

The Hinge of Bridge-Building Leadership is really about relationships. The church's vision to reach people in their community who are lost and separated from Jesus can only be carried out if the church members are serious about befriending these people and gathering them around the cross and empty tomb of Jesus. This is often new territory for many members of the church, and the pastor leads as he scouts out this territory in advance. Once the vision is determined and the goals and strategies set, the pastor then continues to lead by interacting with the residents of this new territory. There he can encourage and equip the members to join him as missionaries on the other side of the bridge. He does this by modeling relationship-building behaviors, some of which are basic to human interaction and others that are specific to the unique setting that he finds on the far side of the bridge.

As the members are encouraged by the example of their pastor and depend on the Holy Spirit, they will move to the next level. We call this the Hinge of Community Outreach, where the church creates opportunities for the members wherein they may practice their emerging art of building bridges. This is the focus of the next chapter.

Discussion Questions

1. Share your notes from last week's community survey activity. What did you learn about your church? About your community? What surprised you about your findings?

2. In what ways can a pastor act as a bridge-builder? As a scout? As a model? How could you help him in each of these capacities?

3. Read Luke 19:5-9. What can you learn from Jesus' encounter with Zacchaeus about building relationships with unchurched people? What kind of people are you most comfortable with? Least comfortable with? Why?

4. Define "friend." Who was the last friend you made outside of your church? Describe how that friendship was made. What is that person's relationship with Jesus? How could you help draw your friend closer to Christ?

5. What are some ways that you personally can fill your Lego with unchurched friends? Where are some "third places" you could hang out to meet new people?

PERSONAL
LEADERSHIP

VISIONARY
LEADERSHIP

BRIDGE-BUILDING
LEADERSHIP

FUNCTIONAL
BOARD

EMPOWERING
GOD'S PEOPLE

FOCUSED
PRAYER

INSPIRING
WORSHIP

MISSIONAL
IMPACT

COMMUNITY
OUTREACH

= PASTOR HINGES
= CHURCH HINGES

8

Community Outreach

How, then, can they call on the one they have not believed in? And how can they believe in the one of whom they have not heard? And how can they hear without someone preaching to them? And how can anyone preach unless they are sent? As it is written: "How beautiful are the feet of those who bring good news!" (Romans 10:14-15).

God has entrusted Christians with the responsibility to search for people who are lost without Christ, and we are to share the good news of what Christ has done. Every generation of the church has the challenge of asking what this will look like in their particular time and situation. As we have mentioned in previous chapters, we are standing at a crossroads in time asking again how the Spirit of God will move through the church to preach the good news. Church consultant and author Kennon Callahan puts it this way:

The day of the local church is over. The day of the mission outpost has come. More precisely, the day of the churched-culture local church is over ... What I am suggesting is that the way in which local churches have done business, conducted leadership, and developed administration is no longer functional in our time. Churches that cling to the old ways that worked so well in the churched culture will survive for a number of years. Their people will grow old together, and many of those churches will eventually die ... The spirit of a mission outpost is one of mission, whereas the spirit of a churched-culture local church is one of maintenance."[1]

While in the past, the "come and hear" approach to preaching the gospel worked effectively, we are now in the midst of a radical shift where Callahan, along with many other church leaders, are observing that we live in a missionary age. This means that the church must shift its gospel preaching strategy to that of being a mission outpost.

Mission outposts are characterized by four qualities. For starters, they assume that the outpost exists for others. It's a declaration that outsiders need to be exposed to the life-transforming truth of the Gospel.

A mission outpost is also an expression of intentionality. Ministering to unchurched people requires effort. As Paul says in Romans 10, how can we expect people to hear about the Gospel of Jesus Christ unless we go out to them? We live in a day that requires us to move out into the harvest, out into the fields.

Thirdly, the reason a mission outpost exists is because it is located within or placed in a mission field. The life of the outpost is surrounded by a world that needs to hear the Gospel announced and see it demonstrated. While in the past, the cultures that needed an outpost were primarily located outside the West, today North America has become one of the largest mission fields in the world. The mission field encircles the local church.

The life of the outpost is surrounded by a world that needs to hear the Gospel announced and see it demonstrated.

Finally, maintaining the mission outpost is secondary to the goal of getting the message out into the mission field. In other words, the management of the church organization is not nearly as important as spreading the news.

Even though Jesus commissioned his disciples to go "to the ends of the earth" (Acts 1:8), many churches today have done just the opposite. Instead of being mission outposts, commissioned to blaze trails on the frontier of a post-church world, many churches see themselves as enclaves where they become insulated from the world. But that's not what Jesus had in mind when he told Peter and the others that he would "build [his] church and the gates of Hades [would] not overcome it" (Matthew 16:18).

In biblical times, the gates of a walled city would have been made out of wood, and they were the most vulnerable point of attack for an invading enemy. The picture we have here in Matthew 16 is that of the city of Hell, where lost people are trapped by Satan. They are condemned to suffer and be tortured for eternity. Jesus the Christ leads his army, the Church, to break down the gates of this evil city to free the hordes of people from an eternity of destruction. And Jesus' promise is that there is absolutely nothing that Satan or his minions can do to stop this heavenly invasion. The church will prevail! The gates of hell will not be able to stop the onslaught of the Gospel.

The Hinge Factor of Community Outreach is all about turning the church into a mission outpost where the army of God is empowered to invade. This is the primary church factor that opens doors and releases people to experiment with ways to reach people with the Gospel.

Empowering Outreach

When consulting with congregations, we generally recommend a minimum of six outreach events and/or activities in their community over the course of a year. When this is implemented, we almost always see a transformative effect on both the church and the community.

St. Luke's Church, located in a medium-sized southern city, was planted fifty years ago to reach people from a German heritage in the neighborhood. The church grew with the rising tide of the suburban sprawl during an era when people came to church to find God.

Now the community around St. Luke's has shifted. One neighborhood is predominately comprised of older, retirement-age people while another is populated by younger families. When Pastor Johnson became the resident pastor at St. Luke's, they shifted to an outward focus. He stated, "Our vision has changed. We're focusing more on young families and youth. We use our facilities differently as now we invite the community to use our space. For example, the state funded a grant that allowed a group of nurses to come here to teach a class about how caregivers could help people with chronic illnesses."

To learn about needs in the community, Pastor Johnson met with the mayor who expressed the desire for mentors of children. As a result, the church adopted a school where they are mentoring and tutoring children. The mayor also connected the church leadership with the local police precinct commander who is willing to work with churches to help the community.

Pastor Johnson shares, "We've also been working with a daycare adjacent to our church property. We've had two Easter egg hunts with their staff, families and children, and we've taken Thanksgiving dinner to them. Our ladies also go to the daycare once a week to read to the children. They love it!" They have also put into motion a 12-week intergenerational Sunday School over the summer, with the first ten weeks similar to a traditional Vacation Bible School program, including arts and crafts, singing and stories. St. Luke's has truly shifted to empowering people to do Community Outreach.

Community Outreach and Net Fishing

The metaphor of net fishing helps us understand the Hinge of Community Outreach. In contrast to pole fishing, where one individual uses a fishing rod to catch one fish at a time, net fishing involves a group of people working together to catch large numbers of fish. The story of the disciples going fishing after Jesus' death can help us see what net fishing in all about:

Afterward Jesus appeared again to his disciples, by the Sea of Galilee. It happened this way: Simon Peter, Thomas (also known as Didymus), Nathanael from Cana in Galilee, the sons of Zebedee, and two other disciples were together. "I'm going out to fish," Simon Peter told them, and they said, "We'll go with you." So they went out and got into the boat, but that night they caught nothing. Early in the morning, Jesus stood on the shore, but the disciples did not realize that it was Jesus. He called out to them, "Friends, haven't you any fish?" "No," they answered.

He said, "Throw your net on the right side of the boat and you will find some." When they did, they were unable to haul the net in because of the large number of fish. Then the disciple whom Jesus loved said to Peter, "It is the Lord!" As soon as Simon Peter heard him say, "It is the Lord," he wrapped his outer garment around him (for he had taken it off) and jumped into the water. The other disciples followed in the boat, towing the net full of fish, for they were not far from shore, about a hundred yards. When they landed, they saw a fire of burning coals there with fish on it, and some bread.

Jesus said to them, "Bring some of the fish you have just caught." So Simon Peter climbed back into the boat and dragged the net ashore. It was full of large fish, 153, but even with so many the net was not torn" (John 21:1-11).

This story provides us with some key principles. The first is quite basic: if you want to catch fish, you have to go fishing. You won't catch anything if you don't go out into the waters of the mission field.

Secondly, we learn how to fish by watching a good fisherman and doing what he does. Fishing is not something that you can learn from a textbook or by going to a class. The best way to catch fish is to learn by doing. Likewise, we learn best how to do outreach by watching others who know what they are doing and then joining them as we are ready and able.

> **We learn best how to do outreach by watching others who know what they are doing and then joining them as we are ready and able.**

Third, you catch more fish with a net than you do with a rod and reel. When multiple people join together, many fish can be caught. In this story, 153 fish were hauled in, a fact which we find unique. It raises the question of why John didn't just write, "They caught a whole slew of fish"? Why is the exact number recorded? Perhaps it is to demonstrate that every one of them was important. Every person is important to God. It's impersonal for us to pray, "God, save all those lost people out there. Amen." Our involvement shifts when we pray, "Save Fred who lives next door and Harry who lives down the street, and use me and my church to help bring them into the boat."

One more observation about the net: With this number of fish, the net should have been damaged. Jesus was the One who orchestrated the entire catch. He is the true "Catcher of Fish," not us. He is the One who reminds us that "faith comes by hearing the Word" (Romans 10:17) and that he will build His church. He is the Word; we are simply the deliverers of the Word. We may be fishermen, but it is the Holy Spirit who truly catches fish!

Fourth, net fishing is an organized enterprise. Somebody has to say, "I'm going fishing," and others have to respond, "We'll go with you" (v. 3). Just as Peter decided to go fishing and invited his friends to go with him, so the spiritual leader of the local church must make "catching fish" his number one priority and then model (Bridge-Building Leadership) what that looks like. You can equip people to fish, you can fish with them, you can tell them where the fishing is good and you can cheer when they catch something. That's the role of leadership in the church with regard to net fishing. At the same time, by helping to recruit, train and organize others to implement the various Community Outreach activities and events, the pastor will also be activating the all-important Empowerment Hinge.

Going Fishing and Vision

The Incarnation was the seminal event of God becoming a human at Jesus' birth. Incarnational ministry, then, occurs when the followers of Jesus demonstrate His love in tangible ways. It is when we become "little Christs" to people who are living apart from Jesus.

But where do you start? There are so many people in our communities who do not know Jesus or are not connected to a local fellowship of believers, and you can't reach all of them. This is why it is helpful to have identified a few critical target segments of the population in the visioning process (Visionary Leadership). Those targets are prayerfully determined on the basis of how readily the people of your church might be able to relate to them. Common ground, people who are not too distant from us culturally, people who have needs which we are most able to address—these are the kinds of factors which go into determining the vision. Of course, you don't ignore people you encounter who are outside the parameters of the vision statement. However the focus lies on the people you envision serving as the starting place.

Incarnational ministry, then, occurs when the followers of Jesus demonstrate His love in tangible ways.

Net Fishing Ideas

1. Service Days

Recruit a task force in your church to spearhead a Service Day in your community. The task force would be responsible for creating a list of one-day service opportunities that are tangible, concrete ways for your people to be a blessing to the community. The possibilities include things like visiting widows, serving local schools, cleaning parks and spending time with people in nursing homes. The point is simple: for one day, people carve out time to tackle a short-term issue. A number of projects could be tackled at once if you have enough volunteers. Some churches even do these service projects on a Sunday during the worship hour to demonstrate to their church members, as well as to the community, that they care more about others than themselves.

2. Challenge Small Groups to Adopt a Need

Small groups that do mission together discover a whole new dimension of connection within the group. A group simply needs to wrestle with this question: "What need in our community (and from our identified target group) could we touch on a regular basis if we banded together?" A regular monthly commitment is a great starting place for the average group.

3. Link with Another Church or Organization

Some fantastic community initiatives may already exist in your area. It's likely that a nearby church or community organization would love to have more volunteer manpower. Partnerships, not done for the sake of proselytizing them into your church, give your people an opportunity to get involved quickly without having to worry about leading or coordinating a project.

4. Re-envision Existing Events and Activities

Rethink the activities and events that you already do well and infuse them with an outward-focused vision. Such events and activities might include Easter and Christmas Services, Trunk or Treat, Angel Tree, Nursing Home Ministry, Educational Classes, Support Groups, Community Meetings/Groups, etc.

Match these activities with the needs of the target group(s) that you are trying to reach. For instance, if you are trying to reach families with young children, events like Trunk or Treat, Easter egg hunts and Christmas programs are natural draws. Remember to obtain contact information of those who come and start building a relationship with at least one of those families.

5. Preach Outreach

Good deeds abound in the Old and New Testaments. Consider emphasizing these aspects of the Christian life for six months so that the congregation gets a steady diet of the idea that God wants them to give their lives away. Sprinkle your sermons with real-life stories of people in and outside your church who are making a difference through serving in the community. Consider encouraging people to give their testimonies, and make sure you give people immediate opportunities to respond. Emphasize a particular outreach activity or event in your message and then have a Connection Card or sign-up sheet for people to indicate their desire to participate. You will be amazed how many people will respond.

6. Triads

Another way to foster Community Outreach is through something called Triads. This is a group of three people who gather regularly in a public setting, possibly a Third Place (see chapter 7). It works best when one person is a committed Christian. The second person should be a seeker or maybe a marginal member of the church. And then eventually you want to add a third person the seeker or marginal church person would bring with them.

A pastor in Alta Loma, California, Neil Cole, began experimenting with this discipleship method about 20 years ago and has now replicated it all over the country and in many parts of the world. The genius of Cole's approach is its simplicity. A group can start anywhere, anytime with virtually anyone. Long doses of training or equipping are unnecessary. The three pillars of his discipleship method are (1) reading large chunks of Scripture, (2) confessing of sins through the use of accountability questions and (3) consistent prayer for the unchurched. When this occurs in Third Places on a regular basis, the life of the group serves as a public expression of the Gospel and can spill over into other conversations.[2]

7. Interest Groups

Examples of interest groups include a sports team, an exercise class, a cooking group, a wine-tasting club or any other activity of shared interest which can be facilitated by someone from your church. And the more unchurch-like it is, the better it connects with unchurched people.

For instance, at one church, there are about 200 people who come every week to a Zumba class. The facilitator begins every session with prayer. She makes it clear that the class is sponsored by the church and that the church cares about its community. She tells the group that the best way to demonstrate that the church cares about them is by praying for them. Then she asks for prayer requests from the group. Only about 20 people of the 200 are a part of the church, but all 20 are using this opportunity to see how God leads them to connect with others.

A church in Arkansas has a paintball interest group. During the regular tournaments they host, trained participants from the church seek to develop relationships. Over the years, they have seen dozens of people, mostly young men, baptized and come to Christ through this interest group.

At another church in Tennessee, a Jewish man came to Christ through a cigar club. My (Terry) wife leads an interest group at our church called English for International Students, through which she has seen many transformed by the Gospel. In another, the pastor is an avid bicyclist, and he leads a group every month on a tour.

In all of these cases, the leader of the group simply took a specific interest or hobby and gathered others around it. And through time, conversations arose where deeper connections were made, trust built and the Gospel shared.

Go for It!

While there are literally thousands of ways to get people involved in net fishing community outreach to share the love of Jesus with the unchurched people in your community, there is one key to them all. You have to do what God is calling you to do. As the church discovers the wants and needs of their community, it will become clear how the church can meet those needs. Your church has unique resources and gifts that can meet specific needs around which relationships can be formed. You are simply looking for the crosspoint of where the needs of your target group and the talents and resources of your own people come together. Wherever that intersection takes place is the starting point for your Community Outreach efforts. Go for it and see where God takes you.

Discussion Questions

1. Based on the imagery of Matthew 16:18, would you say your church is more like a "mighty fortress" or a "mission outpost"? Explain your reasoning.

2. Read John 21:1-11. What are some key fishing principles that are taught in this story? How can those "net-fishing" principles be applied to the Hinge of Community Outreach?

3. Which of the net-fishing ideas listed in this chapter did you like best? What are some Community Service Projects or Net Fishing Events that your church could do in your community? When would be the best time of the year to do these? How could you help "take up the net" to make such an event happen?

4. As an individual or together in your group, take some time right now to pray for these activities and events.

5. Activity for next week:
    One of the richest sources for determining where to begin doing Community Outreach is to interview your community leaders. A thirty-minute interview with a leader in your community will be eye opening. Use the survey below as an interview guide. Consider making a visit to:

    • Local government officials (Mayor, Aldermen, etc.)
    • Public service agencies (Police, Fire, EMT)
    • Planning or zoning office
    • School board, teachers and principals
    • Community service agencies (e.g., Child Protective Services)
    • Health care professionals

Community Leader Interview Questions:

1. What are the greatest strengths of our community?
2. What would you like to see different in our community in 5 or 10 years?
3. What are the three greatest challenges that may prevent these visions from developing?
4. What are the most pressing problems facing people living in our community?
5. How might we (our church) partner with you to improve our community?

PERSONAL
LEADERSHIP

VISIONARY
LEADERSHIP

BRIDGE-BUILDING
LEADERSHIP

FUNCTIONAL
BOARD

EMPOWERING
GOD'S PEOPLE

FOCUSED
PRAYER

INSPIRING
WORSHIP

COMMUNITY
OUTREACH

MISSIONAL
IMPACT

= PASTOR HINGES
= CHURCH HINGES

9

Functional Board

Mary was glad to see a new family with a young child in church late-ly. One Sunday, when the baby started to cry inconsolably, the mother left the worship service to minimize the disturbance. As she walked toward the cry room, Mary followed her to see if she could help in any way. As they entered the cry room, she was shocked by its condition. Without any young families attending church in recent history, the cry room had been neglected. Now it served as a storage facility with only a couple of cold, metal folding chairs for any distraught parents that might happen to come.

This got Mary thinking. She began to work with a few others who wanted to spruce up the cry room, and she donated her comfortable rocking chair. When she brought it to church, she was surprised to learn that the church board would need to approve its placement. In addition, she was told that her spontaneous work on the cry room should have first been approved by the board.

Week after week, the chair sat in a remote corner of the parish hall. Five months later the board approved the placement of the rocking chair, but when they went to fetch it from its hidden corner it had disappeared. Mary had taken it back home. At least now it wasn't needed; the new family with the baby hadn't been seen in church in six weeks.

While this board was comprised of faithful people who worked hard to fulfill their duties, the way that it was organized worked against it being functional. Even more, it worked against the mission of the church. Instead of empowering people to reach people with the Gospel, it actually got in the way.

Church boards play a crucial role in the life of the church. However, like Mary's church, many congregations are stuck with a board that was organized for church life of a different era. And therefore it is not any longer functional. Even though the board in the story above did not act in a helpful fashion, the board members themselves would not have regarded their decision-making procedure concerning rocking chairs as dysfunctional; rather they would have seen themselves as carrying out a sacred trust. The reason for this disconnect is that most of our oversight structures were designed around the needs and values of the members of past generations. When a church sees God's vision to open the church doors outward to seek and save those who are lost, they soon realize that the board must be reconfigured in such a way to fit that vision.

Boards that We Have Inherited

Every board, no matter how it operates, aims to be functional. In our work with churches over the last ten years, we have been impressed by the faithful, diligent board members who give "life and limb" to their churches. Boards may have functioned quite well in previous circumstances, and we too often assume that if they functioned well then that they should do so now. When we begin working with an established church, one of the things we do is to help the leadership think through the board structure that is already in place. Most often it consists of a large number of elected and appointed positions, usually a set of officers and the heads of numerous committees, all stipulated in the bylaws of the congregation. The orientation of the typical church council is to manage, and sometimes micro-manage, the details of the ministry. This type of board structure is based on a bureaucratic model of church governance.

In 1971, St. Matthew's Church adopted a governance system advocated by a widely-respected consultant of the time. The resulting bylaws called for 12 committees, each with its own chairman and budget, responsible for the management of every conceivable aspect of the church's organization and ministry. The governing board was composed of each committee chair, the entire board of elders, three trustees, six officers and a pastor (who was ex-officio), for a total of 26 positions. The congregation did their best to make the system work, even though consensus was hard to obtain with so many people on the council. By 2005, the membership had declined to 50 people, and the leadership had been scrambling for years to fill all the board positions. Henry found himself being President for life, reluctantly running unopposed every three years. Janet was both Financial Secretary and Treasurer, even though everyone knew this was a conflict of interest. Frank wore three hats: Chairman of Outreach, Stewardship Chairman and Head Trustee. Of course the Evangelism and Stewardship Committees each had a membership of one: Frank. But it was no big deal because there was never anything to report at council meetings. Because he was a Trustee, however, Frank did help the pastor replace the broken tap in the ladies' restroom.

This kind of board structure requires the board members to be so involved in managing the details that the big picture of why God has called the church into existence and the priorities of reaching people with the Gospel don't even make it on the agenda. They are just overwhelmed with the needs of the institution. This is not because the board members don't care about the vision of sharing the Gospel. It's simply a ramification of the way that the board has been set up. It is designed to micro-manage details, and in many cases, make sure that those details get done. This approach is no longer feasible in this era of the church.

How Boards Best Function

Church boards or councils are essential to the life of a local congregation, but they must be functional. This occurs when they are viewed within an overall structure of governance that has four levels.[1]

Level 1: Board Oversight

The first level is that of the church board, which operates differently from that found in the bureaucratic model. Instead of a large management group, it is a small group of leaders who are passionate about the church's vision and its implementation in the congregation. We will provide concrete direction for the way such a board operates after we introduce the other three levels.

Level 2: Empowering Pastoral Leadership

At the second level, we find leadership that empowers. In the bureaucratic system illustrated above, the pastor is not expected to play much of a leadership role in the organization. The pastor is to stick to spiritual shepherding while the leadership of the organization is left to the church council.

I (David) was once a part of a consultation team at Calvary Church. During the entire consultation, Pastor Ron sat in the background and hardly spoke a word. After reading the minutes of previous council meetings, we observed that this was his pattern. Interviewing Ron by himself, we found that he had a rather striking vision of where the church could be headed. His silence was not by his choice but was dictated by the expectations of the congregation. In subsequent coaching sessions, Ron came to understand that he did not have to accept this role, and that in a rapidly declining congregation he had little to lose by asserting visionary leadership. Ron was freed up. He started by working with the members who were in charge of the various programs and events at Calvary, helping them reorient these activities as bridges into the community.

Some on the board were inspired; others criticized. Ron pressed on and was able to encourage a passion for lost people in the community.

Eventually they looked at revising the bylaws to fit the vision. Since then, the congregation has experienced slow but steady growth.

The senior pastor is the nexus between the governance board and the leaders who manage the ministries. He is the one person in the organization that is rightly involved in both realms. His presence on the board is not ex officio as staff, but as the leader of the staff. He not only empowers and supervises those who manage the ministries, but, as holder of the pastoral office, is also the inspirational leader on the board. He should not be the Chairman of the Board who runs the meetings and enforces policy, but he is the spiritual leader of the board and the link between the board and the ministry leaders.

> **The senior pastor is the nexus between the governance board and the leaders who manage the ministries.**

The senior pastor will meet regularly with the staff and ministry leaders to cast vision, catalyze ministry that impacts the vision and help them coordinate their work so that it fits into the direction of the church. He will also be the board's voice to those managing the ministries regarding the guiding principles, which will be spelled out below.

Level 3: Ministry Management

Management is the work of key ministry leaders who are led by and are accountable to the senior pastor. This staff of key leaders (whether paid or volunteer) has a good deal of latitude in the management of their respective areas, yet they function within the scope of the established board policy. They work directly with members of the congregation in carrying out activities that have a direct impact on the church's vision.

When we work with a church, we help the pastor identify a group of "people of passion," a core who are inspired by the outwardly-focused vision. In the best case scenario, some of these people will move into positions of ministry leadership. Because these leaders have already been interacting with the pastor in the visioning process, they often quite naturally function in this way.

In addition, there are existing heads of ministries that precede the new vision. As is often the case, the old structure of ministry management does not always line up with the new vision. This is why it is so crucial to involve everyone in the congregation in setting and supporting the vision (see chapter 6). Existing leaders will already be committed to the vision and will understand why they will be facing discomfort when redefining ministry roles.

Level 4: Ministry by All

When the church is organized around the Great Commission of Jesus, every ministry and activity will be designed to involve the members of the church in hands-on service in the community. All do the ministry, not just some who have official positions. The other three levels are designed to support the fourth. This is done in two ways. First, members have venues where they can interface with people in the community. Secondly, members are encouraged and equipped to be effective in forming relationships with individuals in the community and in sharing the Good News. Those on the other three levels must recognize that while they are leaders of the church, they are also members of the church on the fourth level who go into the world and make disciples.

The Functional Board

The functional board lies at the heart of visionary governance. The question we face is "How do we make it functional?"

To answer this question, we must first consider the size of the group. In general, whenever six or more people gather formally, the need arises for some kind of authority structure to keep order. Therefore we suggest to limit the size because a group of up to five or six people can function collegially. By avoiding authority structures and unnecessary complexity, a governance board of limited size will relate to each other infor-

We suggest to limit the size because a group of up to five or six people can function collegially.

mally and thereby economize the time. A small board, together with the senior pastor, will readily form an identity around the vision, which they will cast with one voice in the congregation.

Our second consideration relates to the kind of people on the board. Whether elected or appointed, whether it has term limits or not, getting the right people on that board is crucial. The right people would include those who are above all passionate about the missional vision of the organization as well as willing to give of themselves sacrificially to it, both in terms of time and resources. They must be supportive of the leadership of the senior pastor, though not his rubber stamp, and of exemplary moral character.

Guiding Principles

When the board members meet, they must be concerned with their own spiritual growth as leaders as well as with performing their duties as visionary leaders in the congregation. They need to resist the temptation to get bogged down in management, keeping their attention unswervingly on the vision. Their role is oversight because they are the keepers of the vision, stewards of the policies that govern them.

Since their mode of leadership is guiding, not dictating, their work will be shaped by three sets of guiding principles: Directional, Boundary and Accountability. Let's briefly look at each.

Directional Principles concern the reorganization of the church's ministry around the vision. The board does not need to manage a lot of details, but it does need to clearly articulate where the organization is headed and make judgments about which behaviors and activities will move the church in that direction.

Boundary Principles clarify the distinction between what is on the playing field and what is out of bounds. While directional principles keep the activities in play that are consistent with the vision, here the concern will be particularly on enforcing moral, legal, theological and financial values for all the players.

Accountability Principles have to do with follow-through on the part of every individual who takes responsibility in the organization. In general, those responsible for various projects and ministries are accountable to the pastor, who is accountable to the board for both his own ministry as well as his work as supervisor of the ministry. Often churches find it difficult to hold people accountable for two reasons. First, since churches are largely volunteer organizations, there doesn't appear to be much that can be done about individuals who do not follow through or even do the wrong things. It is difficult to "fire" a volunteer. Secondly, being that the central message of the church is love and forgiveness, it doesn't feel right to put people under the law who are seeking to further the Gospel, even if they are not being effective and are in some cases doing harm to the church's mission.

Even so, without accountability it is difficult to make progress toward the vision. This was the case at Bethany Church where Ben wore many hats on the church council. When he stood to give his reports, he would smile and say, "I report progress!" While this pattern turned into a standing joke, it wasn't really funny, because everyone knew that there wasn't any progress. The board has the responsibility of overseeing ministry effectiveness.

Metrics are an essential part of accountability principles because they can tell us how well we are doing in objective terms. It is easy to measure how many people attend church, how many events are held and how many people attended those events. However, those metrics may not tell us much about progress toward the vision. The board must determine which things are most important to measure and what would constitute effectiveness in each metric as it impacts vision. A church that aims to open doors will celebrate individuals sharing a faith testimony with an unchurched person even if it does not increase the worship attendance. In such a church, an important metric might be the number of new relationships that members formed outside the church, and the number of times

The board must determine which things are most important to measure and what would constitute effectiveness in each metric as it impacts vision.

members shared the Gospel of Jesus with unchurched people. Other metrics could include the number of outwardly-focused events undertaken by the various ministries of the church and the number of people from the community attending those events. One obvious metric frequently overlooked is the number of people, complete with contact information, on the church's prospect list.

Board Meetings

Board members are also church members, and they should be active in the church's ministry along with all the other members in the actual ministry. In other words, they operate at Level 1 and at Level 4. With all we have said so far with regard to board responsibilities, one might imagine a board which meets frequently and for long hours to get it all done. Thus it might seem that involvement on the board might work against actually being involved as a minister. In reality, however, it can be done efficiently in quarterly meetings and some special meetings when needs arise from time to time. John Kaiser in his book *Winning on Purpose* boils everything down to four quarterly meetings that focus on these themes: connecting with Christ (Biblical mission and values), connecting with people (culture and community), updating the guiding principles (accountability and support) and monitoring performance (leadership development). Congregational meetings need only take place once or twice a year and become a time to report and celebrate more than a time to deliberate and decide. Members do not need to be involved in micromanagement any more than the board, and their precious volunteer time should be focused on doing ministry. The important things which would require a vote besides the watershed events of calling a pastor or buying and selling property would be setting the vision and passing a budget prepared by the board.[2]

A board comprised of a few people who are passionate about God's vision for the church can govern in effective and efficient ways to move the whole organization forward in fulfilling the Great Commission of Jesus.

Changing the Board Does Not Come First

The value of structuring along the lines of the four levels is profound. With a lean structure, fewer people are needed in governance and little time is spent in meetings. This system maximizes the time of everybody in the organization for accomplishing the vision with its various goals by concentrating the congregation's resources on the accomplishment of the vision.

In addition to better stewardship of time and resources, the four-level system helps individual leaders discover where their talents and passions may be best put to use. At Bethlehem Church, Sue had served for years as the secretary of the church council. She never got excited about keeping minutes at administrative meetings, but somebody needed to do it, and by doing it, she felt like she had done her service for the church. During the visioning process, Sue went on a prayer walk around the neighborhood and prayed for the courage to overcome her shyness enough to approach a stranger on the street and ask them if they had any prayer needs. Her prayer was not only answered, but the response led to a rewarding conversation and the beginning of a new friendship. Sue was so enthused by this early ministry win that she started gathering people to go on more prayer walks, even after the information-gathering phase of the visioning process was complete.

As a result, prayer walking has become a regular ministry at Bethlehem, and Sue became its key ministry leader (Level 3). She found a new passion in the "doing" part of the mission and wound up being a key leader. On the institutional level, even though the bylaws had not anticipated nor designated a need for a "ministry of prayer walking," Sue's leadership regularly led to the building of many bridges into the community. Sue managed her area of ministry without a standing committee. Each prayer walk was like a task force unto itself. As for her duties as secretary of the church council, the new board would have to figure out who would keep the minutes.

Sue was not the only victim of the bureaucracy at Bethlehem Church. The system was getting in the way of the vision by competing with the church's mission for the members time and attention. At a council meeting, when it was suggested that they needed to rewrite the congregation's bylaws as a consequence of the vision they had so enthusiastically adopted, the level of tension in the room visibly rose. As their coach, I (David) was present, and I realized that revising a constitution would turn all their attention to its structure and away from the vision which must drive the new life cycle. As we discussed in Chapter 6, vision is the driver of a new life cycle for the church, not structure. Also, the potential for conflict in reworking the time-honored system could result in the new vision being overshadowed or even ignored. When we first started working with churches, we instructed churches to deal with church structure and governance issues up front so that they did not interfere with the revitalization process. We learned the hard way that this produces more heat than light, more conflict than hope.

Bethlehem already had a new vision, and they needed to focus on that and reaching goals that moved them toward that vision. With regard to the structure and their board, they needed to behave along the lines of a functional board for the time being, and down the road when some of the details of how they would be organized under the new vision had solidified, they could write some bylaws to reflect it.

Vision launches the people into a new life cycle, and a healthy board structure is one of the supportive components that will hold the vision before the members' eyes and help them understand all of its practical ramifications in the daily life of the congregation.

Vision launches the people into a new life cycle, and a healthy board structure is one of the supportive components that will hold the vision before the members' eyes and help them understand all of its practical ramifications in the daily life of the congregation. An organizational structure with a functional board at its head will develop a set of guiding principles for living out the vision in the congregation. It will also devise systems of accountability so that everyone knows what constitutes success in advancing the vision and how they are doing in reaching their goals.

After coaching the church board at Bethlehem for more than a year on morphing into a functional board, they began to get impatient with the old structure. They knew it was time to start rewriting their bylaws, and by this time they all knew what was needed without my saying a word about it. They were able to make the changes quickly, efficiently and without acrimony. Because they had been operating in the four levels of ministry already, approval was unanimous.

Discussion Questions

1. Share your findings from last week's community leader interviews. What did you learn about your community? What surprised you about your findings? Where do you see an intersection between the needs of your target group(s) and the talents and resources of your church's people?

2. Would you say that your church currently has a Functional Board? Why or why not? If you don't know much about the governance structure of your church, you may want to talk to your pastor or to a current board member.

3. What are the four levels of governance recommended in this chapter? How is each one to function in regard to the others? How well would you say your church functions on each of these levels?

4. What are the three types of Guiding Principles? Describe each one and why they are important. How are individuals responsible for various ministries in your church held accountable? How might this be done differently in a Functional Board system?

5. How does the Functional Board Hinge further the mission and vision of the church? If you think that your church would benefit from a more functional board, what steps might your church take to move toward that reality?

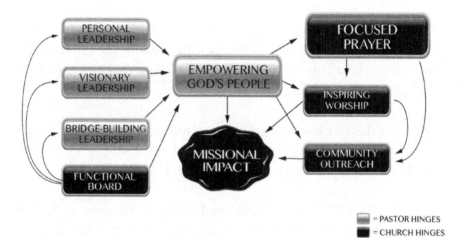

▭	= PASTOR HINGES
■	= CHURCH HINGES

10

Focused
Prayer

Our world is shaped by those who make things happen. We value
those who see a need, assess the steps required to meet that need and
then they get it done. This impacts us all in a variety of ways. Often
we are so shaped by an achievement-oriented mindset that our lives
are overwhelmed by constant, ceaseless activities. Sleep deprivation is a
serious health issue today.

Not only are we hard working, but thanks to all of the cool electronic tools that we can carry in our pockets, we are always connected
and communicating 24/7 with each other. The younger generations illustrate the extreme of our situation. Even when in the same household
or sitting across the table in a restaurant, they often prefer texting over
face-to-face conversation.

Those of us who are leaders in the church are not immune. We
are shaped by the pull of constant activity. Action, action, action. So
we look at the action of Jesus, and we put plans in place to replicate his
actions, to do the work of God.

In the midst of the constant activity, have we lost contact with our
Father, the source and reason for it all? Have we have lost the art of

conversation with the One who deeply loves us? King David's repose, "I have stilled and quieted my soul; like a weaned child with its mother, like a weaned child is my soul within me" (Ps. 131:2). His further instruction to "Be still, and know that I am God" (Ps 46:10) is one we rarely follow. And if we have lost this contact with our Father, then what do we have to offer the lost who don't know Jesus?

In the midst of all of his ministry action, Jesus understood the value of prayer. He knew that he could not do it alone. He understood that he needed to minister out of his communion with the Father (John 5:19). He needed others who would follow his path. At one point of his training of the twelve disciples he told them that the "workers are few" but the "harvest is plentiful" (Matt. 9:37). There are many in our communities who are ready to hear the Gospel, but there are not nearly enough in churches equipped to share the Gospel. In this passage where Jesus proclaimed that the "workers are few," he did not instruct the disciples to get out there and do more ministry activity in order to share the Gospel. He told them to pray for others to join in the work (Matt. 9:38).

All churches pray, but it's prayer that is focused on the lost and unreached and equipping God's people to connect with them that really makes a difference.

Churches that open doors to the community understand the value of prayer, but not just any kind of prayer. All churches pray, but it's prayer that is focused on the lost and unreached and equipping God's people to connect with them that really makes a difference.

Focused prayer directly impacts the Hinge factors of Inspiring Worship and Community Outreach, and these both have a direct relationship to sharing the Gospel.

Prayer that is focused on raising up harvesters and asks the Lord of the harvest to equip his people is the Hinge that opens the church's doors into the community. Churches that pray in a focused way have a missional impact. Church leaders that pray for the Lord of the harvest "to send out workers" transform the world.

Breaking through to Focused Prayer

Focused prayer was a central part of the life of the early church. We see this throughout the stories of Acts. The great responses to the message of the Gospel are directly related to the prayer of God's people. The Apostle Paul wrote about this:

> Devote yourselves to prayer, being watchful and thankful. And pray for us, too, that God may open a door for our message, so that we may proclaim the mystery of Christ, for which I am in chains. Pray that I may proclaim it clearly, as I should. Be wise in the way you act toward outsiders; make the most of every opportunity. Let your conversation be always full of grace, seasoned with salt, so that you may know how to answer everyone (Col. 4:2-6).

Focused Prayer, according to this passage opens doors for the message of the Gospel. It gives us the ability to communicate the Gospel clearly, to have wisdom with those who do not know Jesus. Basically, it empowers us to share the Gospel in compelling ways.

For most in the church, though they know that is important, it remains undone, and when it is done, it remains unfocused. Churches experience barriers to prayer, that if not dealt with, keep churches mired in action without power. These are prayer barriers, and there are six of them that we have observed in our work with churches.

Barrier #1: Prayer is boring.
Barrier #2: Prayer lacks direction.
Barrier #3: Prayer is awkward.
Barrier #4: Prayer doesn't make a difference.
Barrier #5: We don't have the time.
Barrier #6: We don't know how to pray.

One church we worked with broke through these barriers by adopting a quite different way of praying, one that embraced the call to Focused Prayer that aims to reach people with the Gospel. They set up a free coffee and water stand in front of the church, which is located on the main thoroughfare through a rapidly changing first-ring suburb. The idea was to give away a free cup of coffee and a doughnut with an offer to pray.

As a young couple walked by, they scoffed at the offer of coffee and prayer. When about 30 yards away, another man ran up and attacked them. The prayer team was able to get between the attacker and the couple, enough so that they were able to find out what was going on.

The couple, Tara and Josh, had just started dating, and the attacker, Pedro, was her ex-boyfriend. Tara had fled the abusive relationship with Pedro a few weeks prior, and he had tracked her down. After over an hour of trying to diffuse the situation, a few members from the team were able to build trust with Josh and Tara. Even though the couple had originally dismissed the idea of prayer, they were now open to it when they realized that the prayer team would not judge them. The team invited them into the church to get some separation from Pedro who was continuing to make a scene. Within a half-hour, both Tara and Josh approached the altar and kneeled in prayer with team members.

Meanwhile, outside the church, Pedro calmed down enough for the two working with him to make repeated invitations for prayer and counseling, but he soon left. After about an hour, he returned visibly less angry. He apologized to the women on the team for the language that he had been using, and he accepted the invitation to go inside so the team could pray for him. Five men laid their hands on him as they prayed at the altar. God softened his heart, and he left with his head down in contrition holding a Bible.

The Lord wants to mobilize focused prayer like this in all of his churches. He is teaching his people to pray that the doors of the church might be opened again into the community. The pattern that Jesus taught his disciples trains us to pray in a focused way.

Our Father in heaven,
hallowed be your name,
your kingdom come,
your will be done

on earth as it is in heaven.
Give us today our daily bread.
Forgive us our debts,
as we also have forgiven our debtors.
And lead us not into temptation,
but deliver us from the evil one (Matthew 6:9-13).

Let's look at the parts of this prayer, using the teaching of Martin Luther from the *Small Catechism* as a guide.

"Our Father Who Art in Heaven"

Jesus instructs us to start off our prayer by addressing God as "our Father." Consider the following story from one man's life:

Nine men were meeting in a mountain cabin for a planning and goal-setting retreat. The leader asked each to share about what they had been learning about being a father. As each shared, tears welled up. Some were going through very challenging seasons of parenting while others were enjoying times of pure delight. But one thing was apparent: they loved their children. The depth of emotion was quite extraordinary, giving us a glimpse of how God must feel about His children.

About this Luther wrote, "Here God encourages us to believe that he is truly our Father and we are His children. We therefore are to pray to him with complete confidence just as children speak to their loving Father."

God desires us to view him as Father when we begin praying. Jesus consistently called out to God as "Abba" or Father which is a first century Aramaic term of great affection and intimacy.

God desires us to view him as Father when we begin praying. Jesus consistently called out to God as "Abba" or Father which is a first century Aramaic term of great affection and intimacy.

Relating to the Father in this way is crucial if we are going to attain a heart for sharing the Gospel. The Father is compassionate and wants all to be saved. If we see God as a tyrant or a demanding, fear-instilling being, then we will not share the Gospel out of compassion, but out of judgment or fear. God wants us to pray to him as Father so that we might experience him as such and thereby transform us so that we might have his heart for the World.

"Hallowed be Your Name"

"God's name is hallowed whenever His word is taught in its truth and purity and we as children of God live in harmony with it," Luther proclaimed.

One of the biblical word pictures that describes our relationship with God is taken from the world of pottery (Jeremiah 18). God is pictured as the potter, and we are depicted as the clay—His work of art. As we hallow his name, we are encouraged to ponder His reputation as a potter who shapes us.

When we address God in this way, it helps us to remember that he is the potter, and we are the clay. The culture we live in celebrates the notion that we are in control of our destiny. We can and should shape our futures. Our lives are what we make of them. However, if we are not careful, we get caught up in the lie of our day that suggests that we are both the potter and the clay. When we take the time to pray "hallowed be thy name," we are admitting that God is the one in control and that he is the one that shapes our lives.

"Your Kingdom Come, Your Will Be Done"

Luther taught, "God's Kingdom comes when our heavenly Father gives us His Holy Spirit so that by His grace we believe His holy word and live a godly life now and in heaven forever."

Let's consider the potter's wheel again. Before an individual can work with a piece of clay, it must be carefully and painstakingly placed in the center of the potter's wheel. If the clay is off-center, the potter will have an extremely difficult time shaping a cup, jar, or dish.

So it is with our lives, our churches, and our communities. Life is best lived in the center of the potter's wheel. The center of the wheel represents God's best— His will for our lives. Blessed is the church that strives to live in the center of God's will. When we pray that God's kingdom would come and His will would be done, we are acknowledging our desire to live a life that is pleasing to him.

When we pray that God's kingdom would come and His will would be done, we are acknowledging our desire to live a life that is pleasing to him.

Give Us Today Our Daily Bread

Clay needs two things to become something useful: the pressure of the potter's hands and water to keep it malleable.

So it is with our churches. While the Father is keenly aware of our needs, we are encouraged to make our requests known to God. As Luther wrote, "God gives us daily bread, even without our prayer, to all people, though sinful, but we ask in this prayer that he will help us to realize this and receive our daily bread with thanks. Daily bread includes everything needed for this life, such as food and clothing, home and property, work and income, a devoted family, an orderly community, good government, favorable weather, peace and health, a good name, and true friends and neighbors."

A posture of asking keeps us humble and dependent. It is a sure-fire way to help us remember that we are the clay; we are the ones that need the hands of the potter to lovingly shape us and apply water to our souls to keep us malleable. When it comes to opening doors in our church, consider these requests:

• Friends who need God: Remember your friends who need a relationship with God. As you pray for them by name on a regular basis pray that the truths of the Lord's Prayer would become real to them. Pray that they will discover that they have a heavenly Father to whom they can take their needs.

- Wisdom: We need wisdom as we navigate through our day so that we manifest the love of Christ and take advantage of every opportunity to share the Gospel.
- Courage: It takes boldness to reach out in a broken world. Sometimes it is not convenient or you may be apprehensive.
- Love: No greater love has a man than to lay down his life for his friends. Today, your need might be for a greater demonstration of love toward another. Or perhaps you do not feel very loved right now.
- Strength: We need a fresh sense of God's resurrection power pulsating through our veins.

"Forgive Us Our Debts"

Luther wrote, "We ask in this prayer that our Father in heaven would not hold our sins against us and because of them refuse to hear our prayer. And we pray that he would give us everything by grace, for we sin every day and deserve nothing but punishment. So we on our part will heartily forgive and gladly do good to those who sin against us."

In his book, *A Layman Looks at the Lord's Prayer*, Phillip Keller recounts a personal story while watching a Pakistani potter at his wheel.

Suddenly, as I watched, to my utter astonishment, I saw the stone stop. Why? I looked closely. The potter removed a small particle of grit from the goblet. His fingers had felt its resistance to his touch.

He started the stone again. Quickly he smoothed the surface of the goblet. Then just as suddenly the stone stopped again. He removed another hard object—another tiny grain of sand—that left a scar in the side of the clay.

A look of anxiety and concern began to creep over the aged

craftsman's face. His eyes began to hold a questioning look. Would the clay carry within it other particles of sand or grit or gravel that would resist his hands and wreck his work? Would all his finest intentions, highest hopes, and wonderful wishes come to nothing?

Why is my Father's will—His intention to turn out truly beautiful people brought to naught again and again? Because of their resistance, because of their hardness. Why, despite His best efforts and endless patience with human beings, do they end up a disaster? Simply because they resist His will, they will not cooperate, they will not comply with His commands. His hands—those tender, gentle, gracious hands—are thwarted by our stubborn wills.[1]

Sin in our lives is a lot like grit. Sin in many ways represents resistance in our lives to the work of the master potter. He is shaping and molding our lives on the potter's wheel.

The church is to confess and experience forgiveness so that it can offer forgiveness to others. When Jesus taught the Lord's Prayer, he followed it with teaching on the call to forgive others. He said, "For if you forgive other people when they sin against you, your heavenly Father will also forgive you. But if you do not forgive others their sins, your Father will not forgive your sins" (Matthew 6:14-15). One of the ways that we offer the world the Gospel is to forgive others in the same way that we have experienced forgiveness. We pray this part of the prayer so that we remain aware of what the Lord has done for us, and through us, does for the world.

> **One of the ways that we offer the world the Gospel of Christ is to forgive others in the same way that we have experienced forgiveness.**

"Deliver Us From Evil"

Luther wrote about prayer and evil by saying, "We ask in this inclusive prayer that our heavenly Father would save us from every evil to body and soul, and at our last hour would mercifully take us from the troubles of this world to himself in heaven."

After the raw material of the clay has been shaped by the potter, it is prepared to be placed in a kiln to be cured. Heat and drought are a part of the church experience because it is part of the human experience. It is not a question of "will the heat and drought come?" as it is "when will the heat and drought come?" When we get to this portion of the Lord's Prayer we are simply asking the Lord to help us not to crack when the heat comes.

Doing the work of the Lord by being harvest workers will put the entire church in the kiln. The enemy of our souls knows that the church that opens its doors brings light into the darkness. Your Father in heaven wants to give you the supernatural help and strength to endure the fiery ordeal.

Peter reminds us though in 1 Peter 5:8-9 that:

> Your enemy the devil prowls around like a roaring lion looking for someone to devour. Resist him, standing firm in the faith, because you know that your brothers throughout the world are undergoing the same kind of sufferings.

Some of the trials and difficulties that come our way in life are attacks of the enemy. And we are given the biblical command to resist him by standing firm in our faith. James 4:7 instructs us to "Submit yourselves, then to God. Resist the devil, and he will flee from you." The Lord's Prayer is a fantastic reminder about the strength and courage to resist the evil one. The power to resist and to stand firm must come from God, and it is ours to grab a hold of if we will only pray.

Praying to Open Doors

While we can initiate prayer in various meetings that we have as a church—corporate services, small groups, leadership meetings—we also need creative ways that will turn our eyes to our communities so that the Lord's Prayer is spoken in the midst of the world. In hundreds of cities across the globe, ordinary believers are prayer walking through the streets of their communities. They pray while walking, with eyes open for the spiritual awakening God is bringing. In other words, Christians are taking their prayers into the communities where they live. This has become a practical method for praying for God's kingdom to come and for His will to be done.

God's Spirit is helping us to pray in the midst of the very settings in which we expect him to answer our prayers.

God's Spirit is helping us to pray in the midst of the very settings in which we expect him to answer our prayers. We instinctively draw near to those for whom we pray. Getting close to the community focuses our prayer. We sharpen our prayers by concentrating on specific homes and families. Here is a creative way to pray during a prayer walk.

Attempt to keep every prayer pertinent to the specific community you pass through. As you do, you will find prayers naturally progress to the nation and to the world. Use a theme passage of Scripture. Unless God guides you to use another, try 1 Timothy 2:1-8. Many have found it a useful launching point for prayer walking. Verse eight speaks of the important dimension to prayer connected with God's desire that all people be saved. "I want the men in every place to pray." Copy this and other passages in a format easy to read aloud several times during your walk. Each of the following prayer points emerges from this passage:

1. Concerning Christ: Proclaim him afresh to be the one Mediator and the ransom for all. Name him Lord of the neighborhood and of the lives you see.
2. Concerning Leaders: Pray for people responsible in any position of authority—for teachers, police, administrators and parents.
3. Concerning Peace: Cry out for the godliness and holiness of God's people to increase into substantial peace. Pray for new churches to be established.

4. Concerning Truth: Declare openly the bedrock reality that there is one God. Celebrate the faithful revelation of His truth to all peoples through ordinary people (I Tim. 2:8). Pray that the eyes of minds would cease to be blinded by Satan so that they could come to knowledge of the truth.

5. Concerning the Blessing of God: Thanksgivings are to be made on behalf of all people. Give God the explicit thanks he deserves for the goodness he constantly bestows on the homes you pass by. Ask to see the city with His eyes, that you might sense what is good and pleasing in His sight as well as what things grieve him deeply. Ask God to bring forth an enduring spiritual awakening.

6. Concerning the Church: Ask for healing in relationships, that there be no wrath or dissension among God's people. Ask that God would make His people, men and women alike, expressive in worship with the substance of radiant, relational holiness. Ask that our worship would be adorned with the confirming power of saints doing good works in our communities.

One church took this idea of prayer walking and put a unique twist on it. As three teams of two walked and drove to various businesses, they actually talked with business owners, and they were able to collect prayer needs during conversations with 20 different businesses. Each of the 84 businesses in the town was mentioned in a worship service and prayers were offered for their success. Finally, a follow-up post card was sent to each business.

This way of praying can have a huge impact upon a community and upon the church. One church member shared this testimony:

One evening my wife and I were strolling through our neighborhood. As we passed different homes we simply asked God to draw our neighbors to himself. When we got to one home, I had a strange idea pop into my head.

Our neighbor had been clearly wronged by a contractor, and the next day there was going to be a major show-down in a courtroom. So with a little apprehension we walked up to his house and knocked on the door. After exchanging brief pleasantries, I simply blurted out, "Tony, I know that tomorrow is a big day for you, and I was wondering if we could pray for you just a minute." He was visibly moved. I didn't pray long, but I did ask God for justice and for a clear sense that our neighbor would be able to recover his money.

Later in the week, Tony stopped by to report that the judge had ruled in his favor! The point I wish to make is a simple one: the idea of praying for my neighbor happened while we walked past his home. There was something about being out in the street that created the opening in my mind and heart.

Imagine the kinds of stories that will arise in your church and in your community when God moves through your prayers like this. God is at work and our prayers open doors.

Discussion Questions

1. Look up the following Bible passages and discuss what each one says about Focused Prayer: Psalm 131:2; Psalm 46:10; Matthew 9:37-38; John 5:19; Colossians 4:2-6. How does the Hinge of Focused Prayer open the church's doors into the community?

2. Of the six prayer barriers, which have you experienced the most? What might be some ways to overcome those barriers?

3. So often when it comes to prayer, it is easier to talk about it than to do it. The remainder of this section gives several prayer exercises that you can use individually or together as a group. Choose two or three of them and exercise your prayer muscles now.

   • Letter to Dad: Take 10-15 minutes by yourself to write a letter to God with an emphasis on thinking about him as a Father. This is a letter to Dad. What's on your mind these days? What kinds of things are you worried about? What are you excited about or thankful for? How do you feel about your relationship with him lately? Is it close or distant? Tell him about how you feel. Simply use this as a time to talk to God honestly about what's going on in your world. If this is done in a group, ask for a couple of volunteers to share what they have written.
   • Prayer Blitz: Write out as many attributes of God as you can think of (e.g., holy, loving, present everywhere, etc.) and then use them in a simple prayer phrase like:
       - Father, I want to thank you for …
       - Father, I appreciate that …
     If this is done in a group, consider praying in rounds. Have each person thank God for a particular attribute or blessing and then praise him for it. Encourage people to pray more than one time.
   • Daily Bread Prayer: Write out a "Daily Bread" prayer to God.

Use categories like friends who need God, wisdom, courage, love, strength, resources and relationships to frame your writing. You are simply asking God to provide "daily bread" for yourself and others in these various categories. You can share this with others or keep it between yourself and God.

• Confession Prayer: Take some time to allow God to remind you of unconfessed sin in your life. Ask God to bring to mind by His Spirit any area of your life that needs to be confessed and forgiven. Think about each day over the past week. Think about each of the 10 Commandments as ways to jog your memory about possible unconfessed sins. Consider each day and/or commandment and if some sin comes to mind, ask God to forgive you and then move on to the next one. You might want to use a phrase like, "Father, I confess that I have been _____ or I have done _____. I ask that you would forgive me for the sake of Jesus and cleanse me with His blood shed on the cross for me."

4. Activity for next week: Prayer Walking

This is an activity individuals can do on their own, or it can be done together in pairs or as a larger group.

Take 10 minutes to go for a walk. As you walk, ponder the needs, hurts and issues that are present in the lives of the people, homes, shops, schools, etc. that you pass by while walking. Pray for whatever it is that you see or that comes to your mind as you walk. You can pray silently or out loud.

11

Inspiring Worship

Since the church's place within this culture has shifted—a point we have made throughout this book—congregations are forced to wrestle with questions related to its most visible element: weekly worship services. Of course, this is not a new conversation, as over the last 30 years we have seen a litany of proposals regarding how worship should be redone. And in most cases, the focus of the discussion is about worship style.

As the leaders at Bethany Church looked around on Sunday morning and saw only 50 people, all over 50 years of age, they realized that something needed to be done. A counsel member proposed the idea of a "contemporary" service. He argued that a flood of unchurched people in their community would storm through their doors. Because Earl and Lisa had some skills to lead this initiative, they gathered a team and began contemporary worship practices. They had to change the meeting time of their 10:00 worship service to 9:00, and they revised the sign to reflect accordingly: "9:00 Traditional Worship" and "11:00 Contemporary Worship." They printed door hangers and distributed them around the neighborhood. When the first "contemporary" service met, it consisted of the pastor, Earl, Lisa and the "worship team," plus five members who used to come at 10:00 and thought 9:00 was too early. Believing new ideas need time in order to work, they persevered. However, after four months, the same little group attended. There was not a flood of people, and the worship team had exhausted their repertoire.

Even worse, many who preferred the traditional service were angry about changing the service times, and about a third of the congregation left in frustration.

We have found that many congregations are reluctant to engage consulting services such as those provided by TCN because they fear that they will be required to alter their worship style. However, from an outreach point of view, it doesn't really matter what style a church uses—at least not at first—because new people won't come because you offer a different worship style. As we have said many times previously, they will come because we go to them with the love of Christ.

The key is to worship in such a way that people are inspired to go out into the community to share the Gospel of Christ's love.

The primary issue is not about figuring out a way to attract people to our worship services. The key is to worship in such a way that people are inspired to go out into the community to share the Gospel of Christ's love. Such "inspiring" worship serves as a "third rail." Trains formally run on two rails, but without the third rail that is charged with a high-voltage current, the train will go nowhere. Worship is the third rail of the church as it contains all the power to move us out into the community.

Shifting Our Worship Imagination

Through the mid-twentieth century in North America, the worship service was viewed by church members and non-members alike as the centerpiece of the church's ministry. For members, the task of evangelism primarily involved inviting the unchurched to attend church services. In the largely-churched post-WWII culture of the day, most of those not attending church were "de-churched" rather than "unchurched," meaning that the likelihood was high that non-church-attending neighbors knew something about the church and believed that going to church was a good thing that they "should" do. Bringing your neighbors to church 50 years ago was an acceptable practice in the culture, and, though a little awkward, it wasn't all that threatening to be an "inviter." The hope was that if people came to church, faith would come by hearing, and there was good biblical precedent for that. Sermons on outreach encouraged members to invite their friends and neighbors to attend a worship service.

Even though it is obvious that our culture has shifted and the unchurched no longer have an interest in coming with us to our services, this imagination about the role of the worship service endures. In our work with congregations, one of the greatest challenges we face is that of helping people get past the attractional mindset. Instead of going to them, we can attract them to us.

To help people process this, we often ask people to reflect on two basic questions. The first is "What are the best things about your church?" Typical responses involve their being friendly on Sunday mornings and having a pastor who is a "good preacher." While these are admirable attributes, they betray the attractional thinking that the visitor who wanders into their worship service will feel welcomed and hear the Gospel.

The second questions is "What things need to change?" Common answers range from needing better signage on the church building to better communication in the newsletter. Some take this opportunity to gripe about particular members being neglected or how young people are not worshiping like they did "back in the day." The responses almost always point to things that need to be fixed in order to get people back in their worship service.

Sharing the Gospel today requires a shift in our imagination away from this attractional mindset to an inspirational one.

Worship and Opening Doors

Inspiring Worship is an indirect Hinge that helps open doors into the community. Since our mission is among unchurched people in the community, they are by definition not coming to church. Because worship services impact those who attend, they serve as the place where God's people get encouraged, equipped and most importantly inspired to enter the mission fields of their everyday lives. When the people of God gather to pray and to praise the Lord, they receive gifts from God's Holy Spirit, spiritual gifts which empower them to live God-pleasing lives which carry forward God's mission.

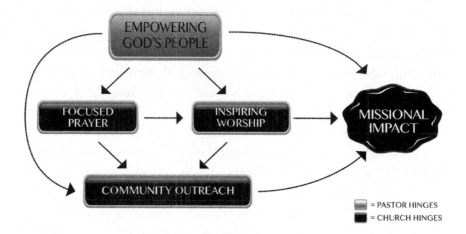

This diagram drawn from our research on spiritual links to mission shows that prayer and inspiring worship have a direct impact on community outreach. In other words, the effectiveness of our outreach efforts is not solely based on our efforts or upon our organizational skills. Through our worship, the Spirit empowers our outreach strategy.

This occurs through giving and receiving. We give ourselves to the Lord as living sacrifices, acceptable because of the once-and-for-all sacrifice of Jesus which removes our sin, and he receives our praises. He gives the power of His Holy Spirit to us, and we receive it in the Word: in Jesus, the Word made flesh, present in the bread and in the cup. We receive God's Holy Spirit so that we may serve as living sacrifices—sacrificing time, comfort and personal priorities and extending ourselves to those who do not yet know Christ.

Worship involves gathering as a community. Inherent in this understanding is the corporate mission of the church which is more than the sum total of the individual ministries of her members. When there is a specific corporate vision, the people of the church gather to receive inspiration and empowerment to own their piece of that calling even as they gather to collaborate.

We can evaluate the success of worship by asking the questions "Did the worshipers receive gracious gifts of God's presence?" and "Were the worshipers encouraged to respond from their hearts with praise and thanksgiving?" A second set of questions focuses on the mission: "Did the worshipers receive empowerment from the Holy Spirit to equip them for their mission?" and "Were the worshipers inspired to give of themselves in Christian service to the community?"

What is "Inspiring?"

While most traditional church members know that faith in Jesus is sufficient for salvation, the excitement about that relationship is often not sufficiently evident in order to inspire them to lead the unchurched to seek a new life in Christ. Church members often testify to the zeal and excitement of recent converts to Christianity which stands in stark contrast to the more mundane expressions of praise among the long-time faithful in the worship service. I (David) understand this well, as someone who was baptized into the faith as an infant and has lived among other believers in the church for many decades. I did however experience a renewal of my faith nearly 50 years ago which stirred up that same kind of new-believer zeal in me, and I have had many other little renewals ever since.

2 Corinthians 4:7 states, "We have this treasure in clay pots." Every believer is a vessel of clay that is filled to the brim with Jesus' Holy Spirit, filled with the gift of faith and with countless other gifts for service. The problem is, though, that we are all "cracked pots," and so we leak.

The harsh realities of daily life crack us up and cause the enthusiasm we have about being children of God to leak profusely. Some day, in eternity, our cracks will be healed, but in the meantime, we need the Spirit of God to constantly refill us with the joy of salvation and the joy of living for him. At the very least, we need that kind of revitalization every week, and I dare say it is the same for the other members of the church that gather for worship.

Defining the "inspiring" can prove challenging because it can involve different things for different people at various times. Yet we know what it is like to be left uninspired, and the longer we remain in that state, the more ineffective our lives become in Christ's kingdom. When "cracked pots" gather weekly, drained of their precious contents, they need to be refilled. This is the most significant purpose of worship. God refills us with His presence and His gifts, and we give him our heartfelt praise.

When "cracked pots" gather weekly, drained of their precious contents, they need to be refilled.

It is a tall order to expect those who lead worship to provide a setting in which all the worshipers are refreshed and inspired on a regular basis. It requires the power and grace of the Holy Spirit. Regardless of the worship style, and perhaps in spite of it, God's Spirit will do the inspiring and the filling. While the task of planning worship involves technical skills and intentionality on the part of those who lead worship, the larger task calls for transparency before the Lord about our inadequacies and prayer that the Lord will have His way among us as we worship. In order for worship to be inspiring, those who lead worship must also be revitalized on a weekly basis, lest this aspect of their work become routine and they rely purely on their human skills.

I (David) have been keenly aware of this in my work with pastors and church leaders. While we are always talking about leadership development and skill building, I realize that there is also a more basic need to balance the work with inspiration. To stretch the analogy, perhaps we could think of the clay pot as a kind of mold, one created in God's image so that when he fills the mold with his gifts, they take the shape of His gracious will. God's grace is everywhere, but without the mold to contain it, its effects are not visible. The work of worship is to present the mold to the Lord; the work of the Spirit is to fill it.

Preparing for inspiring worship, then, requires significant prayer for insight into what will help a particular congregation of worshipers, both individually and corporately, to love God more deeply, understand their calling more completely and motivate them more profoundly to use His gifts for service among the people of their community.

Swedish Pastor Bo Giertz, upon his election as Bishop of Gothenberg in 1949, wrote a pastoral letter entitled "Liturgy and Spiritual Awakening" to his churches. In it, he embraced a necessary tension between "liturgy" and "awakening" in which each belong to a Christian "heritage which we are called to preserve." He describes so well these contrasting components:

> Both liturgy and awakening were found in the apostolic church. They are spoken of already at Pentecost. "Now when they heard this, they were pricked in their heart, and said unto Peter and the rest of the apostles, Brethren, what shall we do?" That is awakening. "And day by day, continuing steadfastly with one accord in the temple" and "Now Peter and John were going up into the temple at the hour of prayer, being the ninth hour." That is liturgy.
>
> … Awakening is like the fire of the Lord which fell upon the water-drenched altar of Elijah, it is the incalculable, sovereign invasion of God which reveals His power among the heathen. Liturgy … is that fire which burns upon the altar in the temple and about which the Scriptures proclaim that it must never be extinguished. Awakening is lightening from above that ignites a new fire. Liturgy is the flame of the Lord already burning among us, lighting and warming the faithful.[1]

"Inspiring" seems to be much like that which Giertz calls "awakening." It is the "invasion of God" which dares to touch the third rail to enliven God's people to be moved by His imminence and to translate, through love and service, that imminence into Christian love for those who do not worship him.

On his way home from work, Steve walked into Our Savior Church on the evening of Ash Wednesday, drained of any spiritual vitality because of the significant cracks in his clay pot. He didn't know why he walked in; he didn't even know it was Ash Wednesday. He saw the lights on in the church, and he intuitively knew that he should go there. It wasn't a particularly dynamic service—no special music, no flowing oratory from the pulpit, no enthusiastic demonstrations from the handful of people in attendance. It was clear, though, that the love of God and the love of those people were palpable. Apart from any liturgical elements of style, this was inspiring worship for him.

Steve's life was changed that evening; his empty vessel was filled, and because it still had cracks, he returned to Our Savior Church for refilling for years to come. Steve wasn't reading inspiration into this setting because of his own great neediness. No worship service at Our Savior was routine; pastor and people alike prayed for and expected the Holy Spirit to take charge of the service, breathing vitality into the ancient words of the liturgy. The majority of prayers he heard there were offered on behalf of individuals the various members knew who did not yet have saving faith in Jesus. The worship service was not all about the attenders. They were intentionally praying for people like Steve, empty vessels looking to be filled with new meaning and purpose. The style of worship at Our Savior was not important to Steve. He was exposed to the heart of God's people there in worship, and that was the time and place the Holy Spirit chose to breathe new life into him.

When Style Becomes Important

Because the worship style is unimportant in attracting new people, if the current style is working for the gathered worshipers we need not attempt to change it. When, however, the members have shared their faith with new people and have begun bringing them to church services with them, the consideration of style will need to be revisited.

Discussions about the style of worship should be shaped by the vision of the congregation (See chapter 6). When a specific segment of the population is designated in the vision as a target group, then part of the strategy would be to develop a worship style which will be engaging to this group. If the mission target is a generation, ethnicity or other people group which has not been historically present in the congregation and is now participating, the question of style is especially important. Here we only speak in generalities, because application can have as many variations as there are local settings. This is a good place for the pastor and the leadership to work with a coach on the specifics.

If the mission target is a generation, ethnicity or other people group which has not been historically present in the congregation, the question of style is especially important.

Two Big Exceptions

There are two exceptions to our premise that changing worship style up front is not necessary. This first exception is related to a mission target of ethnic or immigrant populations where language and/or culture will need to determine style. This kind of ministry is generally a vision option for urban churches, which are often on the downside of their life cycle. At one point in the history of the church which I (David) served in New York City, there were five culture-specific ministries worshiping on our campus in addition to the traditional Anglo congregation. Each was initiated by a leader who was a native of the respective culture and was also seen as a missionary by the Anglo congregation. The worship style in each new mission was very different from that of the traditional congregation, as it was geared to the specific cultural group it was designed to serve. The support these new starts received came not only in the form of a place to meet and finances but also in the prayers and relational support of the Anglo congregation. As people from various countries learned English, many began attending the

English service, and their children caused the long-forgotten Sunday School to restart. Within a few years, the English service had grown in numbers and was eventually attended by people from more than 30 different cultural and ethnic backgrounds.

Worship in the Post-Modern Generations

The other exception to our rule regarding not changing worship up front is a new start or a restart specific to post-modern generations. The 2009 Pew survey revealed that a third of the people born in America after 1975 are unaffiliated with any formal religion. While this is a growing and disconcerting number, there remain a large number of people under 35 who are willing to take the Gospel seriously and will consider affiliating with a church. While many of these people come from families with a Christian background, it is a given that most of them will not want to worship in their "father's church." Elizabeth is a 29-year-old relative of mine (David) who moved to Manhattan because of her work. Raised as a Christian, it was important for her to find a church which suited her needs. I was aware of a couple of megachurches which have been effective in ministering to young adults in Manhattan, but otherwise thought of this borough in the heart of New York City as a pretty hard-nosed and godless place to live. So I was surprised to learn from Elizabeth that throughout Manhattan there are many new churches, some no bigger than house churches, which are entirely comprised of people under 35. Trying a number of them, she admitted that it did feel odd that no "older people" were present in these churches, and yet she would not have considered attending a traditional church.

One of these new post-modern churches in Manhattan is a satellite of the church where I used to serve, which is located in an outer borough of the city. Matt, the 30-something pastor, planted it by networking on social media. He put his vision out in Manhattan cyberspace, and within a few months he had a core of passionate people ready to launch a church. I asked him what he did to make this happen, expecting some details about using social media, but his immediate reply was,

"I prayed like I never prayed before." Matt has his priorities straight; the style must intentionally speak to his generation, but the substance of worship must be inspiring. And there is nothing that brings inspiration like prayer. The style of worship was as different from Earl and Lisa's "contemporary worship" at Bethany church (see above) as it was unlike a "by-the-book" traditional service. Matt's constituents would probably roll their eyes if they saw the "contemporary worship" sign in front of Bethany which they would interpret as "70's boomer music." Twenty years from now a still younger generation may be rolling their eyes at them.

Inspiring Worshipers

Inspiring worship may not seem initially to be about mission, but mission is the result of worshipers who are inspired. Their inspiration comes from God's Spirit as they grow in love for him, which cannot help but manifest itself in abiding love for the people in our world. Ultimately, inspiring worship is a foretaste of the heavenly feast to come where all else shall cease but the eternal, joyful songs of praise for God our Savior. This foretaste of eternity with the Lord is a strong motivation for us to share this enduring joy with those around us. In worship we are inspired to be about the business of doing Our Father's will: the business of bringing people to Jesus. In his instructions on worship, Paul writes to Timothy:

> **Inspiring worship may not seem initially to be about mission, but mission is the result of worshipers who are inspired.**

I urge, then … that petitions, prayers, intercession and thanksgiving be made for all people … that we may live peaceful and quiet lives in all godliness and holiness. This is good, and pleases God our Savior, who wants all people to be saved and to come to a knowledge of the truth (1 Tim. 2:1, 30).

Inspiring Worship, the third rail of the church, contains all the power, and we can touch it and not die, because Jesus already died in our place. Risen and ascended, he continues to lavish gifts of ministry by His Holy Spirit on His church in mission.

Discussion Questions

1. What has been your experience with changing worship styles and/ or times to try to increase attendance? Would you agree that the primary issue is not figuring out a way to attract people to our worship services but to worship in such a way that people are inspired to go out into the community to share the Gospel of Christ's love? Why or why not?

2. How do the Hinges of Prayer and Inspiring Worship affect Community Outreach and ultimately the missional impact of the church?

3. Where and how do giving and receiving occur in worship? How can those aspects of worship be used to evaluate the overall effectiveness of the divine service?

4. How would you define "inspiring"? Using the illustration of a clay pot in 2 Corinthians 4:7, what is the role of worship leaders, as well as worshipers? What is the role of the Spirit? On a scale of 1 to 10 (with 1 being "smashed pots" and 10 being "overflowing buckets"), where would you rate your church when it comes to Inspiring Worship? Where would you rate yourself?

5. When does worship style become important? How does the church's vision impact its worship style? What does that look like at your church?

12

Next
Steps

A few years ago, there was a television commercial promoting Fram Oil Filters. While the spokesman walks around an auto repair shop, a mechanic is overhauling an engine in the background. Then the spokesperson holds up a Fram Oil Filter and says, "The choice is yours. You can pay me now, or you can pay me later!" The message is simple: You can spend just a little more on a premium Fram Oil Filter now, and as a result you can save a lot by not having to spend big bucks later on an engine overhaul.

The only question is: will it be now or will it be later?

Churches today have a similar choice before them. As we have pointed out numerous times in the course of this book, it's no secret that the American church is struggling. Churches like those of Pastor Matt, First Church and Grandma Martha—the stories from chapter 1 that we highlighted—find themselves at a crossroads. Will they keep doing what they have always been doing or will they chart a new path?

The question is: will your church opt for a new path now or will it be later?

For many, the way to find this new path has been to tout exceptional pastors, model churches and ideal strategies with an invitation to mimic their successful programs. While such an approach sounds like it should work, it fails to deal with the real issues that we face. While we hope for a "silver bullet" for church growth or a "magic pill" for revitalization, the reality is that such solutions only provide short-term programmatic boosts. They fall short of actually charting a new path. In our work with churches that have tried this conventional approach, we have discovered that searching for a model to copy, if it happens to work in the short term, only "kicks the can" down the road of time for the next generation of church leaders.

Jesus has not given up on the church, as he promised that he would build it.

But there is another option, a way to lead the church into a new future and into God's promises for God's people. Jesus has not given up on the church, as he promised that he would build it. This approach seeks to empower God's people, God's everyday, ordinary leaders and followers, to create a new way of being the church.

After over a decade of working with such pastors and churches, we have found a way that churches can "pay now" and as a result save a lot down the road by not having to pay much more at a later point.

Transformation

As the name of our organization implies, Transforming Churches Network engages the entire system of the church, including the culture of the community in which God has placed it. No part is considered in isolation from the others, as they are all interrelated. Change in one part affects change in the other parts as well. Hence the importance of all 8 Hinge Factors!

The dynamic power in this change process is rooted in the word transformation. Transformation, by its very nature, requires deep and lasting change (Romans 12:2). Such rarely occurs quickly, easily or without significant sacrifices. At its core, it requires repentance.

Repentance simply means to turn around, to change directions. In the Old Testament, the Hebrew word for repentance is *shuv*, which literally means to turn around. If a farmer is plowing with a team of oxen, when the animals would get to the end of a furrow, he would yell, "*Shuv,*" i.e., turn around; go in the opposite direction. Thus, to repent means exactly the same thing, to turn around, go in a new direction. Turn away from what you are doing and move toward another option.

Throughout this book, we have invited churches to *shuv* from inwardly-focused, self-protective church behaviors and turn toward loving God and loving others by adopting activities and behaviors that take the church out into the community with the Gospel.

When it comes to the transformation of churches, there are both individual and corporate components. It is corporate in that it points the entire church back to its biblical roots as a called out assembly on a mission (1 Peter 2:9). At the same time, this church transformation mirrors the change individual Christians experience in their personal lives of faith. For individuals, there is a grace-initiated change from selfishness to service, from sin to devotion, from worship of self to worship of God. Through the proclaimed Word, people are convicted of sin, comforted with the Gospel and moved by the Spirit to a different way of life.

The transformation for churches occurs, then, as a plurality of people move from being primarily a spiritual club for church insiders to being both a caring assembly and an externally-focused ministry serving others in the name of Jesus Christ. The church therefore seeks to emulate Jesus by serving others rather than to be served or to serve itself (Matthew 20:28).

Merely doing "church" better or getting more people in the pews is not the goal and is not acceptable. Nothing short of deep change or transformation is the true goal. When that happens the church will be different, behave differently, be renewed and improve the way it lives out its calling and ultimately bring more people to Jesus.

Transformation of Patterns

The transformation of individuals and of churches involves the transformation of patterns. For instance, if you try to lose weight, stop smoking or change an addictive behavior, it's not enough to depend upon will power or making a New Year's Resolution. Yes, it begins with commitment and resolve, but there must also be corresponding life pattern changes. This is why there are organizations like AA, Weight Watchers and other support groups. It is also why weight loss, smoking cessation and rehab clinics are billion dollar industries.

Simply wanting to do the right thing is not enough. David Maister, in his wonderfully-titled book, *Strategy and the Fat Smoker*, makes this powerful statement:

> The primary reason we do not work at behaviors which we know we need to improve is that the rewards (and pleasure) are in the future; the disruption, discomfort and discipline needed to get there are immediate. To reach our goals we must first change our lifestyle and our daily habits now. Then we must summon the courage to keep up the new habits and not yield to all the old familiar temptations. Then, and only then, we get the benefits later.[1]

So how do we change our bad habits now so we can gain these wanted benefits later? Award winning New York Times author, Jon Acuff, shares these thoughts on busting up old patterns: "When we're unhappy with one part of our lives the other parts get impacted too. I'm ready to change this pattern in my life. Maybe that's you. … Maybe for you it's not your weight, it's your job. Or your relationships or your finances. The 'fluff' in our own lives can take a million shapes. So how do you break a pattern?"[2]

One way is to engage an expert. In order to lose weight and get in better physical shape, Acuff partnered with a personal trainer to help him put an exercise plan together. He says, "If you want to break a pattern, find an expert."[3]

Malcolm Gladwell, in his book *Outliers*, invokes the 10,000-hour rule which postulates that it takes 10,000 hours of practice with the intention of improving that makes one an expert.[4] The authors of this book have each logged well over 20,000 hours of meaningful "practice" (through research and study, pilot projects, field-testing and feedback loops) over the past decade to discover and develop effective pattern-breaking processes.

Baby Steps

Dave Ramsey, the personal finance guru, talks about getting out of debt in "the same way you learned to walk—one step at a time."[5] For instance, it is much easier to take the baby step of starting a $1,000 emergency fund than to take the giant leap of removing a $100,000 of debt. Therefore, start with small, relatively easy to do tasks, like starting a small savings account for emergencies, and eventually you will be able to completely change your lifestyle and reach your ultimate goal of having financial peace.

What would be some meaningful baby steps related to transforming your church and ministry? To put it another way, how can you build up your hours of meaningful practice toward becoming an expert in opening doors to your community with the Gospel?

How can you build up your hours of meaningful practice toward becoming an expert in opening doors to your community?

One way to jump-start the process is to take advantage of the 20,000 hours of practice that we have logged. Instead of reinventing the wheel, use something that is tried and true, and you will begin to establish a clear path for your baby steps.

For instance, we have developed a workbook entitled *Skill Builders: Leadership Tools for Opening Doors to Your Community*,[6] which provides practical skills tied to each of the eight factors introduced in this book. While there are many important leadership skills that are needed to lead a church effectively, these eight focus on the areas that actually open doors and turn churches around. In addition, these are eight skills that can be applied in any kind and size of church.

Another baby step we have developed is a Hinge Factor Assessment Survey.[7] Congregation members take an online survey in about 15 minutes, and it gives insightful feedback on how they score their pastor and their church on the eight Hinge Factors.

Consider, for example, the case of a small, stagnant church located on the far western edge of the Ozark Mountains. With an average age of 72, the congregation was known in the community as the "church for old people." However, after taking some baby steps, the congregation took up the challenge of reaching young families with the Gospel. They planned a special week of summer camp activities for children. The members developed their own lessons and activities. To help ensure maximum participation, they provided meals and snacks. The summer program concluded with a Mexican dinner and mariachi band concert. The whole community was invited.

To prepare for the crowd, members were asked to park in a vacant field across the road. They used golf carts (one of the perks of having elderly members in your church!) to ferry members to the door. The paved parking lot at the church was reserved for guests. When a local restaurant heard of the event, they volunteered to donate the tacos, rice and beans for the meal. The members donated the dessert. With over 500 people in attendance, this was the single largest event in the church's history. Over 80 prospects were identified. The congregation is building on this success with a weekly afternoon camp experience for children. More than that, the church is now thriving and growing and is no longer viewed as just a "church for old people."

The Path to Transformation

We have tested various ways for churches and pastors to take steps that will change their habits, so that they can effectively utilize the Hinge factors that open the doors to their community. These components of this path include:

1. Consultations—Interventions where experts give specific pre-scriptions for change
2. Coaching
3. Learning Communities
4. Resolve to Start the Process
5. Choose a Good Partner

Consultations

Consultations are weekend events where a team of trained "experts" meets with congregation members, leaders and staff to assess the congregation's ministry. The team then makes recommendations on what changes are needed for the church to become more outward focused. The weekend event is preceded by a congregational self-study, several surveys and assessments that help the team gather and analyze significant data provided by the congregation.[8]

Our research and experience show that consultations are the fastest way to get congregations to become more outward focused and begin engaging their communities with the Gospel. It jump-starts the basic three-stage process of learning a new pattern.

The first stage is unfreezing, brought about by adequate discomfort or disequilibrium in order to produce sufficient survival anxiety in the organization. In a congregational setting, people recognize their "sin" and become anxious about whether or not their church will die if they continue on their current path.

What becomes necessary in this change process is for learning anxiety to be reduced by providing a viable way forward.

In the second stage, there is a neutral zone where learning, transformation and change can occur. This second stage is characterized by learning anxiety, which involves both un-learning old self-serving or sinful habits and learning new habits, both in terms of behaviors and thinking in their faithfulness to God's will. Resistance is often experienced at this stage, where there is pressure to stay the same or return to what is old and familiar and maintain homeostasis, even when intuitively people know it is not best or right.

The third stage is called refreezing where the new behaviors are reinforced and adopted as the new norm. What becomes necessary in this change process is for learning anxiety to be reduced by providing a viable way forward. This reduction in learning anxiety is often created by things like a compelling vision, formal training, coaching, role models and support groups, which together create what sociologists term psychological safety.

Consultations are designed to initiate a real change of behavior in the whole of the organizational system rather than just trying to increase organizational efficiency or improvement. The consultation needs to be a sufficient "shock to the system" to unfreeze the organization of the church. It is truly "good, right and salutary" then to diagnose the concerns of an internally-focused church while also prescribing the "fixes" necessary to create an externally-focused ministry. This will look different in each church, but the goal is the same: repentance, transformation and real change versus simply improvement or greater management efficiency.

If you are interested in a consultation, read through Appendix B to determine if this would be appropriate for your church.

Coaching

An even more indispensable element for breaking old patterns and nurturing the transformation process is coaching. "Coaching is the art and practice of guiding a person or group from where they are toward the greater competence and fulfillment that they desire."[9] "Coaching is helping people grow without telling them what to do."[10]

The coach leads pastors to the green pastures of the Word, reminding them of the importance of their own spiritual vitality, provides support through the transformation process and, like any good helping relationship, the coach holds the pastor accountable and suggests key resources to begin to change old patterns into new helpful behaviors.

The coaching process helps pastors leverage their strengths to better reach the community with the Gospel. When pastors receive customized, personal support from a good coach, they are equipped to brainstorm, problem solve and work on the church's Hinges. In addition, they can begin to help their own church leaders become change agents who will, in turn, become more effective in equipping others in their ministry sphere to reach out with the Gospel.[11]

When pastors receive customized, personal support from a good coach, they are equipped to brainstorm, problem solve and work on the church's Hinge factors.

For more about the coaching we provide through TCN, read through Appendix C.

Learning Communities

Since deep change is so difficult, pastors need support and skill development in order to effectively empower God's people for works of service. A great way to provide both peer support and practical learning is through a pastors' Learning Community. Learning Communities are collegial, regionally-based small groups of pastors, ideally between eight and twelve individuals, which meet monthly with the purpose of developing and honing leadership skills related to church transformation. Because most pastors are well prepared as theologians, worship leaders and caregivers, the focus of Learning Communities centers on leadership development.

By participating in one, pastors will develop skills that will help empower others through a variety of ways:

- Peer Support. Members of the learning community will "be there" for each other in very tangible ways: praying, developing strategies and sharing resources.

- Accountability. The collegiality of a learning community encourages its members to plan, commit to and put into practice behaviors that lead toward transformation in a pastoral, fraternal context.
- Learning from Experts. The members of the pastors' Learning Community come to a meeting prepared to discuss a book or article, which covers some aspect of the transformation process.
- Adult Learning Format. Just-in-time training works best for adults as opposed to just-in-case training. This is the modern version of the old lesson, "Use it or lose it!" Adult learners will focus on what they feel will be the most useful to them, so each group will take the topic of each session in its own unique direction.
- Best Practices. Each session of the Learning Community curriculum includes homework assignments designed to bring the principles of transformation into a practical focus in the personal and professional lives of the participating pastors.

One Learning Community participant shared, "Pastor's gatherings were extremely helpful. As the group discussed the lessons, we each made contributions so that the understanding of the group was greater than the understanding of any single person. In a [church] that has lost its mission, it was helpful to hear what was happening in other congregations that were trying to be missional. I also enjoy the sense of not being alone as my congregation and I are making these major changes."

The goal is to empower people for works of service. This transforms the people and the church as a whole. And it transforms pastors so that they can think, live and lead in empowering ways. A pastor who participates in a New York Learning Community admitted, "The Pastor's Learning Community is huge because we need to change before the congregation will change. The Learning Community is the place to get all the tools, insights and training to lead in a new way as well as the encouragement to do it from others going through the same."[12]

Resolve to Start the Process

Engaging in a consultation, finding a good coach and joining a Learning Community are all great processes to receive the necessary support to begin breaking old patterns and start revitalizing your church and ministry. Certainly, there are others as well. What's really important at this point is that you simply resolve to start the process.

The nature of the challenge of starting the process can be illustrated from the medical world. After experiencing shortness of breath, chest pains, etc., a person goes to the doctor for tests and finds out that there is significant blockage of the arteries surrounding the heart. The "technical fix" is open-heart surgery and life-long medication. However, everyone knows that unless there is a corresponding lifestyle change in the way the individual eats, exercises and manages stress, the heart disease will soon reoccur. And yet, a large majority of the population will not change their lifestyle and simply rely on the "expertise" of the surgeon and the power of the medication, only to have the heart disease return or even suffer a fatal heart attack a few short years later. Changing the individual's lifestyle is the real challenge.

The mission of the church calls for a lifestyle approach, believing that we must go much deeper to understand what it means to lead our churches in new ways.

We see these same kind of lifestyle challenges in the pursuit of weight loss or trying to stop smoking or drinking. Again, David Maister reminds us, "If you don't understand from the beginning that you have to change your lifestyle, now and forever, then you are wasting your time."[13]   Simply dabbling at self-improvement, reducing your cigarette or alcohol intake to half of what it used to be, or cutting out a few calories by drinking diet sodas (as an antidote to eating pie!) will not cure your smoking habit, alcoholism, obesity or whatever it is you are trying to change. "You are either seriously on the program, really living what you have chosen, or you are wasting your time."[14]

In much the same way, the mission of the church calls for a lifestyle approach, believing that we must go much deeper to understand what it means to lead our churches in new ways. This calls for resolve, commitment to the journey. We must go far beyond simply diagnosing and analyzing existing problems and trends. Real leadership helps people face problems that require new learning and change if their church is to thrive anew. Real leaders push us beyond our current expertise and ways of doing things.

Find a Good Partner

We have found that changing the way we do ministry is nearly impossible to do by ourselves. That is the primary lesson learned from Weight Watchers, AA and other support groups. Thus, church leaders who are serious about leading the church down a new path recognize that the most important asset is to have someone "walk alongside" of them while they are implementing the difficult and challenging changes necessary to engage a post-church culture and community with the Gospel.

Let us suggest that you find a good partner in your transformation process. Such a partner should have a good track record and provide excellent resources and training, not just for the pastor but also for church leaders and members, as well as on-going coaching and equipping for pastors.

The goal, then, is to find a partner and a process that equips church leaders (pastors and laity) with knowledge and skills that will enable you to think and act "adaptively," i.e., you need to be able to help your congregation face the pain of change and navigate through the complexities of living out the mission of God in our post-church culture. You need a process that will help you identify the root causes and issues so that you aren't simply dealing with symptoms that will initially seem to be resolved, but then later, return.

So wouldn't it be great if somehow you could combine all these fine ideas and principles into one comprehensive process that is biblically based, research tested and affordable for most congregations? If you believe that to be the case, then you will be interested in learning more about TCN's Seasons of Discovery.

Seasons of Discovery is a step-wise church transformation process delivered in four seasons over two or more years that helps churches begin to effectively engage their community with the Gospel. This process, developed by TCN after working with a 1,000 churches in the United States and Canada, takes all the revitalization principles that we have learned over nearly a decade in the trenches of church transformation and combines them in one comprehensive package.[15]

Get Started

Back when I (Terry) was growing up on the farm, my Dad used to say, "Don't just stand there, do something!" The point is clear. If you want to accomplish anything worthwhile, you have to get started doing it. And what could be more worthwhile, indeed eternally important, than being instruments of Christ in opening doors to your community for the Gospel?

The tendency, of course, after reading this book is to put it down and not really do anything differently. If you don't believe me, take a look at the dozens of books that you have in your office, church or home right now and then mentally make a list of how they fundamentally changed your life. The reality is that probably none of them made a significant difference. This book won't either, but the Holy Spirit can, if you resolve right now to start doing some things differently.

The choice is yours. Do you want to pay now or pay later? Will you take seriously Jesus' command to "go and make disciples of all nations," and experience the joy the angels feel whenever even one sinner repents? By investing yourself and your congregation in a church revitalization process now, you can be sure that, by God's grace and power, there will be those that will not have to pay later for their sins in hell, because they will come to know the One who has paid for everything by giving His life for us all.

Discussion Questions

1. Based on what you have read in this book, are you more inclined to choose a new path now or pay later?

2. What is the meaning of "repentance"? How do both individual and corporate repentance impact church transformation? Look up the following Bible passages and share what they have to say to you about church transformation: Romans 12:1-2; 1 Peter 2:9-10; Matthew 20:28.

3. What are some ways to begin breaking old, unwanted patterns? What would be some meaningful baby steps when it comes to transforming your church and ministry? Based on the "path to transformation" recommended in this chapter, where would be a good place for your church to start?

4. How strong is your resolve to get started breaking old patterns and start revitalizing your church and ministry? What will you do to keep that resolve strong?

5. What do you plan to do as a result of reading this book and discussing these questions today? Next week? Next month? Pray that God will help you to follow through on your blessed intentions.

Appendix A
Pastor's
Time Log

The pastor's time log form provides a one-week snapshot of how you are using and allocating your time. Please use the categories on this overview to summarize how you have spent your time this week when you are filling in the spreadsheet. Please note that some categories may not be applicable at this time, depending on where you are in the revitalization process.

Empowering God's People
  Suggested goal: 5 hours/week
  Ways to accomplish this:
    • Preparation for upcoming training opportunities
    • Running or participating in training workshops/events
    • Coaching or mentoring appointments with staff or other lay volunteers

Personal Leadership
  Suggested goal: 2 hours/day
  Ways to accomplish this:

- Prayer, bible reading, journaling, fasting, solitude, exercise
- Reading leadership material

Visionary Leadership
Suggested goal: 5 hours/week
Ways to accomplish this:
  - All communication tools and meetings
  - Planning, goal setting and reviewing of calendar
  - Working with congregational resistance
  - Sermon preparation (if directed toward an outward-focused vision)

Bridge-Building Leadership
Suggested Goal: 8 hours/week
Ways to accomplish this:
  - Friendship cultivation with unchurched people & others who do not know Christ
  - Time invested in building relationships with community leaders and organizations

Community Outreach
Suggested goal: Varies
Ways to accomplish this:
  - Recruiting and training outreach leaders
  - Assessing and identifying community needs
  - Planning and implementing net-fishing events and service projects
  - Incarnational ministries

Functional Board
Suggested goal: Varies
Ways to accomplish this:
  - Selecting the governing team, training the team, writing guiding principles, setting goals and strategies

Focused Prayer

Suggested goal: 2 hours/week

Ways to accomplish this:

- Prayer meetings, training
- Support for outward-focused prayer

Inspiring Worship

Suggested goal: 3 hours/week

Ways to accomplish this:

- Worship service planning and preparation (if directed toward attracting new people and/or incorporating incarnational ideas)
- Recruiting and training worship leaders

Maintenance: Institutional

Suggested goal: 3 hours/week

Ways to accomplish this:

- Meetings, Bible studies, confirmation, sermon & worship preparation (if not directed toward an outward-focused vision)

Maintenance: Member Care

Suggested goal: 3 hours/week

Ways to accomplish this:

- Counseling, emergencies, interruptions, visitation, etc.

Time	Mon	Tues	Wed	Thur	Fri	Sat	Sun
6-7:00	Devotion	Devotion	Devotion	Devotion	Devotion	Devotion	Devotion
7-8:00	Breakfast	Breakfast	Breakfast	Breakfast	Breakfast	Breakfast	Breakfast
8-9:00	Planning	Secretary	Sermon	Sermon	Pray Tm		Worship
9-10:00	Staff Meeting	B Class	Sermon	Sermon	Stew Dir		Worship B Class
10-11:00	Staff Meeting	B Class Planning	Sermon	SS Dir	Counsel	Net Event	B Class Worship
11-12:00	Office	Planning	Sermon	Assim Dir	Counsel	Net Event	Worship
12-1:00	Lunch	Joe G	Jim B	Debbie	Lunch	Lunch	Jones
1-2:00	Hospital	Workout	Hospital	Workout	Home	Workout	Jones
2-3:00	Hospital	Office	Hospital	Office Out Dir	Home		Nap
3-4:00	Con Pres	Planning	Coffee	Out Dir	Home		Kids Park
4-5:00	Con Pres Home	Planning Home	Coffee	Conf	Home		Kids Park
5-6:00	Home	Home	Home	Conf Home	Home		Home
6-7:00	Home	Home	Home	Home	Date Wife		Home
7-8:00	Bud Mtg	Pray Tm	Wor Mtg	Home	Date Wife		Home
8-9:00	Bud Mtg	Read	Wor Mtg	Read	Date Wife	Sermon	Planning
9-10:00							
Total							

Emp God People	Per Lead	Vis Lead	Bridg Lead	Comm Out	Funct Board	Foc Pray	Insp Wor	Main: Inst	Main: Care	Total
	3.5									3.5
1		1				1		3		6
2								4		6
2		.5		1				2.5	1	7
1		1		1				3	1	7
			3	1						4
	3		.5						2	5.5
				.5				1	2	3.5
		1	1	.5	1					3.5
		.5	1		.5			1		3
								.5		.5
	1						1	1		3.5
	2	1				1	1	1		5
6	9.5	5	5.5	4	1.5	2	2	17	6	58.5

Time	Mon	Tues	Wed	Thur	Fri	Sat	Sun
6-7:00							
7-8:00							
8-9:00							
9-10:00							
10-11:00							
11-12:00							
12-1:00							
1-2:00							
2-3:00							
3-4:00							
4-5:00							
5-6:00							
6-7:00							
7-8:00							
8-9:00							
9-10:00							
10-11:00							

Emp God People	Per Lead	Vis Lead	Bridg Lead	Comm Out	Funct Board	Foc Pray	Insp Wor	Main: Inst	Main: Care	Total

Appendix B
Is Your Church Ready for a Consultation?

How do you make an informed and prayerful decision on whether to seek a consultation from an outside advisor for your congregation? Based on our experience with having conducted hundreds of consultations across the country, we know the basic criteria that qualify a congregation for a successful consultation. Here they are:

1. Is the church strong enough to have a consultation? It is important to understand that consultations will create some stress for the church because it produces change, and change always puts pressure on the status quo. In fact, there will be some people who simply can't tolerate this stress, and the only way they can resolve it is by leaving. For this reason, we generally don't recommend consultations for congregations with less than 75 in worship attendance, have little or no cash reserves or have a history of internal conflict.

   Please note the word "generally" above. There are always exceptions to these rules of thumb. For instance, we have heard of a church that had a very successful consultation that had only 25 people in attendance. Of course, they also had an endowment fund of $4 million. They were "strong" enough to withstand a little financial stress if a few people decided to throw in the towel and leave. The deal breaker for them would have been refusing to spend a substantial portion of their Rainy Day Fund to love their community by helping those in need.

2. Is the pastor truly committed? Notice that we're not asking if the pastor should be committed, although he may feel that way at times. However, it is vitally important for the senior pastor to be totally committed to the revitalization process and thus, the consultation, as well. Of course, it isn't just the pastor who needs to be committed to the process. The leaders and members should be as well. However, without the senior pastor's leadership, modeling and influence, it is difficult to move forward.

How do you know if your pastor and congregation are truly committed to a church transformation process? Here are some questions for the pastor and church leaders to ask themselves that will help determine an accurate answer.

   a. Do you recognize the need for change?
   b. Are you willing to change your primary focus from internal to external?
   c. Are you willing to embrace your leadership role?
   d. Are you open to changing the pastor's role to one of empowerment?
   e. Are you willing to be held accountable?

We provide a survey for pastors and also one for church leaders. How pastors and leaders score on these surveys give a good indication of your church's readiness to have a consultation.

3. Is the church adequately prepared for a consultation? There are

some important elements that should be in place prior to a consultation that will help to insure a good experience. In addition to the points made above, these would include:

a. Start engaging in some door-opening activities prior to the consultation. Recruit some mission-minded people who will provide leaven for the transformation process. Even in very stagnant congregations, it is not difficult to find a small group of passionate people who are longing to see God touch the world in a personal way. Just look for people who have a passion for Christ, a passion for their local church and a passion for their community. Get them started in some simple door-opening activities like prayer walking, community surveying, service projects, outreach events and natural evangelism. We have developed a resource entitle *People of Passion* that helps jump start this. The ripple effects of these activities will spread to others within the church while also opening new doors for the Gospel into the community.

b. Get spiritually prepared. The transformation of a church really is a spiritual exercise (cf., Romans 12:2). Thus, it is essential to be spiritually "in shape" for such a process. In addition to the pastor and church leaders, all of whom should be people of prayer; it can be very helpful to organize a separate prayer team, which would regularly bring the petitions generated by the transformation process before the throne of grace. This should be happening in the months prior to the consultation as the congregation considers whether or not to engage a consultant. Of course, once that decision is made, the group should continue and even intensify its efforts just prior to and during the consultation itself. This could also include a day a week of fasting by leaders and church members.

Saying that you want a consultation and being ready for one are not the same thing. Doing trumps good intentions every time. For instance, in the Parable of the Two Sons, Jesus commends the first son who refused his father's request to go and work in the vineyard but ultimately changed his mind and did the work; and he chastises the one who initially agreed to work but didn't follow through (Matthew 21:28-31). If you are willing to have someone from the outside take a hard look at where you are now, help you put together a plan for the future and help you regularly evaluate your progress, then a consultation could be the best thing you ever do.

Appendix C
Coaching
Makes a Difference
by Scott Gress

The costs and challenges of coaching have led some who are involved in the process of revitalization to consider cutting costs by cutting out the coaching. My experience with this strategy makes obvious that the revitalization process doesn't work without coaching. We are creatures of habit and in our sinfulness and stuckness we tend to avoid the tough stuff. Coaching is an indispensable part of the hard task of revitalization.

But change doesn't have to be so difficult. With coaching it can get easier instead of harder. Coaching, while it involves a financial cost and the challenges of facing difficulties and changing behaviors, can produce rewarding and God-pleasing results. Coaching ensures accountability to the prescriptions of the consultation weekend and facilitates the working through of what we have identified as the eight core competencies to change and revitalization. Coaching in our process is also about support, encouragement, celebration and love.

It is lonely slogging through the day-to-day demands of ministry. Not too many people really understand the highs and lows of dealing with the fallout of the human condition that pastors have to face. Pile on top of that the emotion and challenges of a plateaued or dying church, the challenges of learning to do it differently for the purpose of revitalization, and it gets exponentially harder. Yet when coaching is introduced there is someone who comes alongside the pastor to "hold up their hands" much like Aaron and Hur in Exodus 17.

As I have coached pastors through revitalization, some lessons have become clear, and I have identified some best practices for coaches in these situations. Coaches who work with pastors in a revitalization process need to:

1. Believe in the person being coached. There is discouragement with any person who is facing decline. Often they have done everything they know to do and are getting nowhere. Many want to throw in the towel. Through faith in God, the coach can have confidence that God will bring His grace to bear on God's servant.

2. Be reliable with integrity. That means the coach will show up for the coaching prepared, on time and ready to give their best effort.

3. Hold the person being coached accountable with love and support rather than condemnation and contempt. Nothing will happen with a manipulative coach. Christian coaching at its heart creates a "grace space" to allow change to blossom and grow. "A bruised reed he will not break, and a smoldering wick he will not snuff out" (Isaiah 42:3).

4. Pray. The coach regularly prays for the person being coached in his own prayer life but also with them in the coaching session. This points us to "the Father of compassion and the God of all comfort, who comforts us in all our troubles, so that we can comfort those in any trouble with the comfort we ourselves have received from God" (2 Corinthians 1:3-4).

And what will be the results? We are finding that when these steps are followed, and good coaching is added, there are more people giving praise to God on Sunday morning, angels are rejoicing over the baptisms of children and adults and formerly discouraged members are finding that God can use them in powerful ways to make an eternal difference in the lives of those who have not yet come to saving faith. In short, congregations are being revitalized, fear is evaporating, and hope is returning. As one pastor said, "Coaching made ministry fun again."

Notes

Chapter 2: Hinges that Open Doors to the Community
[1] See Eric Siegel, *Predictive Analytics* (Hoboken, NJ: John Wiley & Sons, 2013) for more information on this kind of research.

Chapter 4: Empowering God's People, Part 2
[1] Ronald A. Heifetz & Marty Linsky, *Leadership on the Line: Staying Alive through the Dangers of Leading* (Boston: Harvard Business School Press, 2002), 111.
[2] Ron Hall and Denver Moore, *Same Kind of Different as Me* (Nashville: Thomas Nelson, 2006).

Chapter 5: Personal Leadership
[1] Robert Quinn, *Deep Change: Discovering the Leader Within* (San Fransisco: Jossey-Bass, 1996), 34-35).
[2] For more information on how to take this survey, visit the TCN website.
[3] For more information on how to obtain a TCN Coach, go to http://transformingchurchesnetwork.org.
[4] Quinn, 45.

Chapter 6: Visionary Leadership
[1] George Bullard, *The Life Cycle and Stages of Congregational Development*, 2001. Accessed at http://sed-efca.org/wp-content/uploads/2008/08/stages_of_church_life_bullard.pdf on Monday, September 14, 2015.
[2] Andy Stanley, *Visioneering: God's Blueprint for Developing and Maintaining Personal Vision* (Colorado Springs: Multnomah, 2012), 17.
[3] A complete plan for conducting a Visioning Day can be found in Chapter 3 of Terry Tieman, *People of Passion: Activities for Opening Doors to Your Community* (Cordova, TN: Transforming Churches Network, 2012).

Chapter 8: Community Outreach
[1] Kennon L. Callahan, *Effective Church Leadership* (San Fransisco: Jossey-Bass, 1990), 22-23.
[2] Details about these "Life Transformation Groups" can be found in Cole's book, *Cultivating a Life for God* (St. Charles, IL: ChurchSmart Resources, 2014), or at his website, www.cmaresources.org.

Chapter 9: Functional Board
[1] The four levels of church structure have been adapted from two resources, John Kaiser, *Winning on Purpose* (Nashville: Abingdon Press, 2006) and Les Stroh and Kurt Bickel, *Structure Your Church for Mission* (Orlando, FL: Strobican Publishing, 2010). These are recommended reading for those who are leading churches into a new life cycle.
[2] Kaiser, 148.

Chapter 10: Focused Prayer

[1] Phillip Keller, *The Inspirational Writings of Phillip Keller* (Nashville: Thomas Nelson Publishers, 2001), 205-206.

Chapter 11: Inspiring Worship

[1] Clifford Giertz, "Liturgy and Spiritual Awakening," http://gnesiolutheran.com/giertz-liturgy-spiritual-awakening/. Accessed on Sunday December 6, 2015.

Chapter 12: Next Steps

[1] David Maister, *Strategy and the Fat Smoker* (Boston: Spangle Press, 2008), 4.

[2] Jon Acuff, "I'm tired of losing the same 30 pounds over and over again," http://acuff.me/2014/12/im-tired-losing-30-pounds/December 29, 2014. Accessed Monday, September 14, 2015.

[3] Ibid.

[4] Malcolm Gladwell, *Outliers: The Story of Success* (New York: Little, Brown and Company, 2008), 35ff.

[5] Dave Ramsey, "Take Control of Your Money One Step at a Time," www.daveramsey.com/new/baby-steps/. Accessed Monday, September 14, 2015.

[6] Terry Tieman and Dwight Marable, *Skill Builders: Leadership Tools for Opening Doors to Your Community* (Cordova, TN: Transforming Churches Network, 2012).

[7] http://transformingchurchesnetwork.org/shop/core-competencies-survey/

[8] For more information on what a TCN Consultation entails, go to our website, www.transformingchurchesnetwork.org, and click on the Consultation icon.

[9] Gary Collins, quoted in Tony Stolzfus, *Leadership Coaching: The Disciplines, Skills and Heart of a Christian Coach* (Virginia Beach: VA: Transformational Leadership Coaching, 2005), 7.

[10] Ibid., 33.

[11] To find out more about getting a TCN Coach, please visit the TCN website.

[12] To inquire about a TCN Learning Community meeting in your area, or online, go visit the TCN website.

[13] David Maister, 5.

[14] Ibid.

[15] For an extensive understanding of how Seasons of Discovery works and how it will benefit your church, visit the TCN website.

About the Authors

Terry Tieman served parishes in Michigan and Arkansas prior to serving as Mission Executive of the Mid-South District for 13 years. He became the Executive Director of TCN in January 2009. His experience as a parish pastor, mission executive, congregational consultant and coach, Learning Community facilitator, and training consultants and coaches, brings a skill set and perspective which informs and directs the work of the revitalization team. Terry lives with his wife, Becky, and is a father to three sons.

David Born served as a parish pastor in New York City for 30 years, where he developed considerable experience in cross-cultural ministry. The last seven of those years, he served concurrently as the Mission Executive of the Atlantic District LCMS, recruiting and training leaders to initiate over a dozen ethnic-specific missions. In 2009, David began work with TCN as the Director of Field Services. In that role, he was tasked with tracking results of the TCN process nationally and assisting specific districts in a hands-on way with consultations, coaching and Learning Communities. Until his death in 2015, he lived with his wife, Anita, in central New York state.

Dwight Marable has been intimately involved with evangelism outreach in 25 countries where exponential conversion growth has occurred. He has led seminars and conferences that have equipped over 25,000 leaders in Asia, Africa, Latin America, Europe, the former Soviet Union, Canada and the USA. Dwight is drawing upon his experience and research in evangelism to enhance the outreach potential of congregations and districts throughout North America by helping them focus on outreach as their primary purpose in God's kingdom. Dwight lives with his wife Linda in the Nashville area.

TRANSFORMING
CHURCHES NETWORK

Is Your Church Ready To Open Doors?

Hinge Events During these one-day events, we discuss the eight "Hinge factors" for church revitalization and help churches discover creative ways to open new doors into their communities.

Learning Community These are collegial, regionally-based small groups of pastors, which meet monthly with the purpose of developing and honing leadership skills related to church transformation.

Coaching Trained coaches support pastors through problem solving, directional equipping and work on the church's "Hinge factors."

Consultations Designed to identify specific issues and give recommendations to the congregation with regard to its ability to reach out to unchurched individuals in its community with the Gospel of Jesus.

Seasons of Discovery This unique discovery process focuses on renewal and healthy transformation. Through four flexible phases, you will be led in a comprehensive, two-year process that will help you discover new ways to reach out to your community.

www.tcnprocess.org

19:10
PROJECT
TRANSFORMING
CHURCHES NETWORK

The 19:10 Project will help your congregation identify barriers for growth and provide recommendations to move past them, in order to reach unchurched people in your community with the Gospel of Jesus Christ.

When partnering with The 19:10 Project, you will receive a unique report containing steps that will help your congregation work together to effectively implement your outreach plan in your community.

Your Unique Report will provide you with:
- Strengths of the congregation which can be leveraged for effective outreach activities and behaviors
- Areas of concern that could inhibit effective outreach
- Prescriptions to address each of the concerns
- A plan with goals and milestones for effectiveness

After your 19:10 Weekend, the project does not end. It continues according to your needs and desires. Upon acceptance of the Weekend Report, your 19:10 team will walk alongside you every step of the way. This includes:
- A trained coach who works with the pastor to help him grow as a leader
- A process to hold the pastor and lay leaders accountable for the changes recommended by the 19:10 team and accepted by the congregation
- An opportunity to discover the church's unique vision for its community
- Bible studies, sermons, outreach resources and leadership training
- Praying like you have never prayed before

www.tcnprocess.org

S E A S O N S O F

DISCOVERY

What is Seasons of Discovery?

- A step-wise transformation process
- Delivered in 4 seasons over 2 or more years
- Easily integrated into the parish calendar
- That helps congregations engage their community with the Gospel

---

Each Season Includes:

- A Personal Coach to Assist the Pastor in ...
  - Planning the details of the season
  - Growing in personal leadership skills
  - Developing effective congregational leaders
  - Assessing results

- Tools for Equipping People for Ministry
  - Sermons & Bible studies
  - Leadership training for the laity
  - Small group resources

- Outreach Activities
  - Practical experience & training
  - Service projects & net-fishing events
  - Opportunities for participation by everyone

w w w . t c n p r o c e s s . o r g

CPSIA information can be obtained
at www.ICGtesting.com
Printed in the USA
LVOW05s0454120117
520661LV00002B/2/P